# Hiring by THE BOOK

### Copyright 2019 by Alan Balmer

All rights reserved. No part of this book may be reproduced, stored in a retrieval system, or transmitted by any means, electronic, mechanical, photocopying, recording, or otherwise, except for brief passages in connection with a review, without written permission from the author.

## About the Author

Balmer earned a B.A. degree in Accounting at The University of Missouri-Columbia and a B.A. degree in Pastoral Ministries at Central Bible College in Springfield, Missouri. Balmer began his career as an Accountant & Auditor in the field of public accounting, has worked as a Human Resources Manager, and is currently employed in the staffing agency field. Balmer enjoys speaking to high school students to provide some of the information contained in this book, with the objective of helping them understand what the expectations will be when they enter the workforce.

## **Acknowledgements**

For this book I wish to thank two influential spiritual leaders that, although they don't know me on a personal basis, have significantly impacted my walk with the Lord through their teachings, sermons, and written works.

First, to Neil Kennedy, thank you for inspiring me to foster the entrepreneurial spirit that I've always known existed within me. I haven't always been sure how that entrepreneurial spirit would work itself out, but your inspiration through Fivestarman (Fivestarman.com), your weekly webinars, and your written works (especially *God's Currency: The Entrepreneurial Drive*) have certainly spurred me on to greater works in the realm of business.

Second, to Bill Johnson (bjm.org), thank you for your powerful sermons and insightful books. They have been instrumental in shaping me spiritually. Your love and promotion of marketplace ministry has helped me to understand that people in business have an opportunity to reach people for Jesus Christ that some others could not reach as easily. Thanks for helping me to understand how I can achieve great results for the Kingdom of God. Your books, especially *When Heaven Invades Earth*, have impacted me profoundly.

In order for you to be made aware when I am going to publish the several books that are currently in the works, please subscribe to my page at:

www.subscribepage.com/j8c0g8

As a gift for subscribing to this page, I'll email you periodic, free, unpublished writings.

You can find out more about other books I've written on my website,

www.alanbalmer.net

Additionally, please feel free to contact me at the email address below for any questions you may have.

Email:
alan.scott.balmer@gmail.com

Scripture quotations marked MSG are taken from *THE MESSAGE*, copyright © 1993, 1994, 1995, 1996, 2000, 2001, 2002 by Eugene H. Peterson. Used by permission of NavPress. All rights reserved. Represented by Tyndale House Publishers, Inc.

Scripture quotations taken from the New American Standard Bible® (NASB), Copyright © 1960, 1962, 1963, 1968, 1971, 1972, 1973, 1975, 1977, 1995 by The Lockman Foundation Used by permission. www.Lockman.org

# Contents

| | |
|---|---:|
| Hiring by THE BOOK | 1 |
| **Introduction:** | 7 |
| **Chapter 1:** RELIANCE ON OTHERS AND SEEKING ADVICE | 23 |
| **Chapter 2:** OUTLOOK, COUNTENANCE, AND DISPOSITION (JOY) | 28 |
| **Chapter 3:** INTELLIGENCE/QUEST FOR KNOWLEDGE, INSIGHT, AND WISDOM | 35 |
| **Chapter 4:** CONTENTMENT (PEACE) | 41 |
| **Chapter 5:** CONFLICT AVOIDANCE AND RESOLUTION (SELF CONTROL) | 45 |
| **Chapter 6:** DILIGENCE AND EXCELLENCE (FAITHFULNESS) | 48 |
| **Chapter 7:** TIMING, CONTRIBUTION, AND CONTROL | 52 |
| **Chapter 8:** THOUGHTFULNESS (PATIENCE) | 56 |
| **Chapter 9:** ARROGANCE ABOUT BEING WRONG | 58 |
| **Chapter 10:** RECONCILIATION (KINDNESS) | 60 |
| **Chapter 11:** GREED AND ETHICS (GOODNESS) | 64 |
| **Chapter 12:** CONTEMPLATION FOR THE RIGHT ANSWER | 68 |
| **Chapter 13:** GOOD NEWS AND BAD NEWS; WINNING AND LOSING | 71 |
| **Chapter 14:** RECEIVING CORRECTION, ADVICE, COACHING, AND REPROOF | 75 |
| **Chapter 15:** HUMILITY | 78 |
| **Chapter 16:** LANGUAGE | 81 |
| **Chapter 17:** THE TRUTH AND ETHICS | 84 |
| **Chapter 18:** GOSSIP | 88 |
| **Chapter 19:** TEMPER (GENTLENESS) | 91 |
| **Chapter 20:** THE BEST IN QUALITY AND SERVICE | 94 |
| **Chapter 21:** BALANCE | 97 |
| **Chapter 22:** REPUTATION | 101 |
| **Chapter 23:** ASSOCIATIONS | 104 |
| **Chapter 24:** CRISIS MANAGEMENT | 108 |
| **Chapter 25:** RESPECTING AUTHORITY | 111 |
| **Chapter 26:** LISTENING | 115 |
| **Chapter 27:** CUSTOMER/CLIENT SERVICE | 118 |
| **Chapter 28:** COMMUNICATION SKILLS | 121 |
| **Chapter 29:** FOSTERING TEAMWORK AND DEMONSTRATING (LOVE) FOR OTHERS | 124 |

| | |
|---|---|
| **Chapter 30**: THE ART OF CONVINCING THROUGH PATIENCE | 129 |
| **Chapter 31**: BRIDGING THE GAP | 132 |
| **Chapter 32**: INITIAL REACTION | 136 |
| **Chapter 33**: TAKING ACTION WHEN NEEDED | 140 |
| **Chapter 34**: DISCIPLINE AND TERMINATION | 143 |
| **Chapter 35**: LEADERSHIP TRAITS | 147 |
| **Chapter 36**: LEADERSHIP PLANNING | 150 |
| **Chapter 37**: SELECTING ONLY THE BEST CANDIDATES AND APPLICANTS | 152 |
| **Chapter 38**: COACHING AND TRAINING YOUR WORKERS | 157 |
| **Chapter 39**: ENSURING ACCOUNTABILITY FOR YOUR DIRECT REPORTS | 159 |
| **Chapter 40**: NAVIGATING CONFLICT | 162 |
| **Chapter 41**: LEADING DEEP AND WIDE | 164 |
| **Chapter 42**: WEEDING OUT THE WICKED | 167 |
| **Chapter 43**: WORKING UP THE LADDER | 169 |
| **Chapter 44**: PLAYING FAVORITES | 173 |
| **Chapter 45**: INSPIRING YOUR TEAM | 176 |
| **Chapter 46**: CARING ABOUT WHAT OTHERS SAY ABOUT YOU | 178 |
| Conclusion: | 180 |

# Introduction:

I have made my fair share of poor hiring decisions throughout 25 plus years of working in Human Resources and Temporary Staffing Agencies. One of my most difficult situations was when I had to terminate an extremely nice and spiritual person who just wasn't performing to the expectations of the position. After attempts at coaching and training this employee, it just wasn't working out. In hindsight, had I known about and used all the tools and resources outlined in this book (which translated into the development of an interviewing methodology and guide that I personally use), I most likely would not have made the hire. Historically, I tried to rely on a gut feel during an interview. By gut feel, I mean how much I felt like myself and the other interviewers connected with the candidate. However, sometimes gut reactions lead us down the wrong path.

As I look back over people I've hired that didn't work out, in hindsight I can see certain skills, qualifications, knowledge, capabilities, and capacities that were missing which would have signaled to me that this candidate was not the correct hire.  All that has changed with the wisdom and insight I've gained as I've walked through what the Scriptures have to say about the categories listed in this book...skills, qualifications, knowledge, capabilities, and capacities.

   My journey down the path of understanding Biblical insight into making better hiring decisions began during a year where I felt impressed to read the Psalms and Proverbs from the Message Bible (MSG).  The Message Bible is not a literal translation but seeks to put the essence of the Scriptures into modern day terminology.  Historically, I've done my readings and study from the New American Standard Bible (NASB) which is a literal translation.  During this new adventure of reading the Proverbs and Psalms in the Message Bible, I would also read the same chapters/verses in the New American Standard Bible to make comparisons.

As I began reading the Proverbs in the Message Bible, Scriptures leading me to clarity regarding making great hiring decisions began popping out at me from the text.  In fact, on the 15th of the month while reading Proverbs chapter 15, in the span of about 45 minutes, I documented in my journal what became the first 15 chapters of this book.  When I first realized that the number 15 was at the core of my launch into this new interviewing and screening process, I first thought that it might just be a coincidence.  Days later, I felt compelled to do some research on the Biblical references and meaning behind the number 15.  Ultimately, what I discovered is that the number 15 has significant meaning.  At the end of my period of discovery, I uncovered Biblical accounts, documentation, and insight showing that 15 has a theme that includes redemption, freedom, restoration, and deliverance.  In the rest of this introduction, I'll list out some of these Biblical accounts with their related meanings.  However, for you as a business owner, executive, manager, or leader who has hiring decision responsibility, the main takeaway for your organization is that, if you will use the tools in Hiring By THE BOOK and only bring in the best candidates, your organization or business can unleash redemption, freedom, restoration, and deliverance from the effects of the pattern of poor hiring practices and decisions you may have made in the past. Hiring by THE BOOK will give you the tools and resources needed to improve your screening, interviewing, and selection process.

**The Significance of the Number 15:**

1. The Israelites in Egypt.

**(NASB) Numbers 33:1-4** These are the journeys of the sons of Israel, by which they came out from the land of Egypt by their armies, under the leadership of Moses and Aaron. **2** Moses recorded their starting places according to their journeys by the command of the Lord, and these are their journeys according to their starting places. **3** They journeyed from Rameses in the first month, on the fifteenth day of the first month; on the next day after the Passover the sons of Israel started out boldly in the sight of all the Egyptians, 4 while the Egyptians were burying all their firstborn whom the LORD had struck down among them. The LORD had also executed judgments on their gods.

The Israelites were enslaved, trapped, and held in bondage by the Egyptians. They were in this situation for hundreds of years. God delivered the Israelites from the bondage of Pharaoh in Egypt on the 15th day of the first month. The Israelites experienced freedom from the oppression and constraints placed upon them in Egypt. Your business or organization may be experiencing some of the same type of entrapment issues due to poor hires that have been made. Usage of the Biblical principles outlined in this book will provide you with a greater advantage in escaping the bondage of poor workers as you head to the promised land of great hiring practices.

2. Esther and the Jews.

**(NASB) Esther 9:18** But the Jews who were in Susa assembled on the thirteenth and the fourteenth of the same month, and they rested on the fifteenth day and made it a day of feasting and rejoicing.

The Jews had a proclamation issued against them for their destruction. An official decree was made by the king where they resided giving permission for non-Jews to kill all the Jewish residents. Through a series of events, within which Esther was prominently used by God, the Jews were delivered from death and destruction. On the 15th day of the month the Jews feasted and rejoiced for the deliverance that had been provided. Their position and status had been restored and they now experienced freedom. Freedom from the fear of bad hires, as well as deliverance from poor hiring practices, can be your future as you implement the strategies outlined in this book.

For a fun study on leaders who had no business being in a leadership position, try researching the book of Esther regarding the king's right hand man, Haman. Haman is the one that incited the king to issue the decree setting forth the annihilation of the Jews. You'll see issues such as pride (I deal with the issue of pride right out of the gate in Chapter 1) that were part of Haman's makeup. In the chapters of this book, you'll find some ways to dig deep in an interview to see if pride might be part of a candidate's DNA.

3. Hezekiah and his illness.

**(NASB) 2 Kings 20:1-7** In those days Hezekiah became mortally ill. And Isaiah the prophet the son of Amoz came to him and said to him, "Thus says the LORD, 'Set your house in order, for you shall die and not live.'" **2** Then he turned his face to the wall and prayed to the LORD, saying, **3** "Remember now, O LORD, I beseech You, how I have walked before You in truth and with a whole heart and have done what is good in Your sight." And Hezekiah wept bitterly. **4** Before Isaiah had gone out of the middle court, the word of the LORD came to him, saying, **5** "Return and say to Hezekiah the leader of My people, 'Thus says the LORD, the God of your father David, "I have heard your prayer, I have seen your tears; behold, I will heal you. On the third day you shall go up to the house of the LORD. **6** I will add fifteen years to your life, and I will deliver you and this city from the hand of the king of Assyria; and I will defend this city for My own sake and for My servant David's sake."'" **7** Then Isaiah said, "Take a cake of figs." And they took and laid *it* on the boil, and he recovered.

Hezekiah was in a position where he was going to die. After an intense period of seeking the Lord regarding his healing, Hezekiah was rewarded by God in the form of a 15 year extension of his life. Hezekiah was being liberated, freed, and restored from his illness and impending death.

For your business or organization, a sickness and/or impending death could be in your future if you allow the wrong employees to become part of your team. Having the wrong employees can lead to loss of customers, teamwork, and can ultimately result in the demise of your organization. By utilizing the Biblical strategies outlined in this book you can begin the process of working toward freedom and liberation from the potential of poor hires that could infect the culture of your business or organization.

4. Hosea and Gomer.

**(NASB) Hosea 3:1-3** Then the LORD said to me, "Go again, love a woman *who* is loved by *her* husband, yet an adulteress, even as the LORD loves the sons of Israel, though they turn to other gods and love raisin cakes." **2** So I bought her for myself for fifteen *shekels* of silver and a homer and a half of barley. **3** Then I said to her, "You shall stay with me for many days. You shall not play the harlot, nor shall you have a man; so I will also be toward you."

Hosea's wife abandoned him and left. Ultimately, Hosea had to redeem his wife, Gomer, from the poor life decisions she had made. The price of redemption Hosea paid for Gomer's restoration was 15 shekels of silver and a homer and a half of barley. Freedom from Gomer's immoral lifestyle was achieved as a result of the redemptive work that her husband Hosea performed.

Utilization of the Biblical tools in this book could be the redemptive work that you need performed in your business or organization in order to turn the corner to freedom and restoration.

5.  Resurrection of Lazarus.

**(NASB) John 11:17-18** So when Jesus came, He found that he had already been in the tomb four days. **18** Now Bethany was near Jerusalem, about two miles off;

While in Jerusalem, Jesus was notified that Lazarus had died in Bethany. Ultimately, Jesus made the journey from Jerusalem to Bethany and raised Lazarus from the dead. John 11:18 says that he traveled 2 miles...a descriptive footnote indicates that the distance was actually measured in the Greek term of stadia. The Greek distance was 15 stadia. The restoration of Lazarus's life was achieved after traveling 15 stadia.

Traveling the path of learning and implementing the Biblical principles in this book could very well be the key to resurrect your business or organization.

There are other examples of the number 15 being representative of redemption, freedom, restoration, and deliverance. However, I think the 5 examples listed so far show you that there is a powerful significance to the number 15. The bottom line is that, as a hiring decision maker or business owner, you want to make sure you take advantage of every tool and resource that is available to ensure you are only bringing in the right and best candidate for every position for which you are recruiting.

What follows in the chapters of this book are Scriptural principles primarily from the book of Proverbs for you to examine as you reflect on your hiring practices. This book is not intended as a legal document authorizing you to ask any question you want during the interview process. You must still observe and adhere to all local, state, and federal guidelines regarding hiring laws.  This book does not in any way infer or state that you should operate outside of those guidelines.  You should always seek professional legal advice to ensure the interview and hiring methodology you employ is in compliance with all laws and that your practices are without any hint of discrimination.

Your work, your business, your leadership role, and your occupation is a place of importance as it relates to both the spiritual and non-spiritual components of your life.  Use your resources and time wisely to ensure that you only hire the right and best candidates for your organization.  I pray that for anyone who reads this book that your personal, professional, and organizational future days will be exponentially better than your former days.

The ultimate outcome of considering implementation of the Biblical principles that follow in this book is to make the best hiring decision you possibly can.  Does using the principles in this book, mined out from Proverbs, mean that you will be able to hire the perfect person every time? Will you always hire someone who achieves 100% in each of the categories that I will outline later in this book? In most cases the answer is no. However, if you are able to determine areas of weakness, deficiencies, and shortcomings about the candidates you will be interviewing, you can make a good hiring decision along with a plan that you can put in place to develop that new hire from day one of the onboarding process. Setting expectations, creating a training plan, and implementing accountability measures before, during, and after the onboarding process is a critical step to ensure you maximize your potential for success.

Each chapter of this book will represent a skill, qualification, knowledge, capability, or capacity that may be important as you consider who you need to hire. Keep in mind that each position you hire for may have a different combination of categories for which you need to interview and screen. You shouldn't feel it necessary or required to go through every single topic, question, or category outlined in this book. Each position for which you recruit, screen, and interview should, however, have some structure in place to ensure the best opportunity for success.  You should definitely, as you go into the interview, have a game plan for the direction you are headed.  By game plan, I mean which of the topics in the chapters that follow will you want to ask the corresponding interview questions.

Regarding the skills, qualifications, knowledge, capabilities, and capacities listed in the chapters ahead, the first 32 chapters deal with categories that are general in nature and can be applied to both the leadership and non-leadership positions for which you are recruiting.  Beginning at chapter 33, for the remainder of the book, you will read about categories that are exclusively geared toward those leadership positions for which you are interviewing.

Lastly, as it pertains to this book's introduction, I want to share one additional item that I discovered during prayer, reading, study, and preparation.  That one additional item is, when I walked through the guidance from the book of Proverbs, I came to the realization that there were links and parallels to what is identified as the fruit of the Spirit in the book of Galatians, Chapter 5 verses 22-23.

**(NASB) 22 But the fruit of the Spirit is love, joy, peace, patience, kindness, goodness, faithfulness, 23 gentleness, self-control; against such things there is no law.**

As such, nine of the chapter titles will incorporate, in parentheses, the name of the fruit that is linked to the nine spiritual fruit listed in Galatians 5:22-23. I do not believe it is an accident that the fruit of the Spirit is linked to nine of the topics that are outlined in the chapters that follow. I believe this is further confirmation, wisdom, and insight that leads, guides, and directs us in understanding that we must have the right employees on the team.

As you journey through this book, I pray that your mind and spirit will be enlightened in the same way mine has been as I've implemented these principles. I've listed my contact information on the pages prior to this introduction. If you have questions please feel free to contact me.

# Chapter 1: RELIANCE ON OTHERS AND SEEKING ADVICE

Proverbs 15:12 The Message (MSG) **Know-it-alls don't like being told what to do; they avoid the company of wise men and women.**

Proverbs 15:22 The Message (MSG) **Refuse good advice and watch your plans fail; take good counsel and watch them succeed.**

As I reflect back over the decades of my professional career, a few names race through my mind as I consider the topic of people who thought they knew it all. I have been in meetings, discussions, and conversations where these "know-it-alls" dominate, have a very strong opinion on any and every topic, and generally foster a spirit of frustration. It became problematic to obtain any meaningful resolution or outcome due to their lack of listening, contemplative efforts, and reflection. Unfortunately, know-it-alls tend to bring a spirit of disunity, lack of teamwork, and division to a business or organization. Does this mean that these individuals can't bring any value to the team? No. However, sifting through the good, the bad, and the ugly that know-it-alls bring to the table can be an exhausting process that drains energy, consumes time, and requires the allocation of other resources in your business or organization.

At some point in the past someone shared with me the following saying that is a great illustration and life lesson.

*God gave us two ears and one mouth. We should listen twice as much as we speak.*

I try to apply this life lesson in order to make sure I grow as a person, leader, and employee and not just spew out everything I know to try and impress those around me. I'm quite aware that I don't know everything and that I ought to try and soak up, sponge, and absorb all I can from others that have greater knowledge than I.

In the interview and discovery process, I like to make efforts at determining if the candidate has any process, system, or network they use to seek advice, wisdom, or counsel in making decisions. Making inquiries of the candidate regarding the last time they sought out a subordinate or peer for their guidance and counsel is a good way I approach the subject. If a candidate cannot cite how they rely on their team to make good decisions, I might be able to conclude through additional questioning that they have a spirit of superiority, to the neglect of the gifts, skills, and talents that their team members possess. I also like to make inquiries of candidates regarding the last time they sought out those in authority over them for their guidance and counsel. I want to be able to make a determination if the candidate has the overall capacity to seek out, receive, and apply sound wisdom, guidance, and counsel.

Ultimately, hiring someone who brings a haughty, proud, and vain spirit or superiority complex to the workplace can result in an overall decrease in productivity for the team by creating low morale. Consider some of the questions listed below that you might use during the interview process in order to make the discovery about how your candidate seeks advice.

- Describe the process, system, or network you use to seek advice, wisdom, or counsel in making decisions.

- Tell me about the last time you went to a subordinate to seek their input for guidance and wisdom.

- Tell me about the last time you went to your manager or supervisor to seek their input for guidance and wisdom.

- For this role, describe the amount of input you will want from the person to whom you will be reporting.

- What is the most difficult decision you have had to make recently?

- When we ask your supervisor or manager this question, how will they respond? "Would you characterize (candidate) as a know-it-all? How has (candidate) demonstrated the ability, capacity, or receptivity to seek out, receive, and apply knowledge, wisdom, and insight from supervisors, subordinates, or peers?"

# Chapter 2: OUTLOOK, COUNTENANCE, AND DISPOSITION (JOY)

> Proverbs 15:13 The Message (MSG) **A cheerful heart brings a smile to your face; a sad heart makes it hard to get through the day.**

> Proverbs 15:15 The Message (MSG) **A miserable heart means a miserable life; a cheerful heart fills the day with song.**

Through the years while working in the staffing agency business, I have been on many sales appointments and cold calls. Of these visits, I can recall some of the businesses where the person at the front desk/reception either lifted my spirit or brought me down. Regardless of your outlook and mentality toward those that have all or a portion of their work responsibilities dedicated to sales, you really don't want your front desk/reception person looking and acting like they were dipped in vinegar; displaying a sour face. Quite literally, your gatekeeper affects the atmosphere of your business or organization. Having the right person as the gatekeeper or front desk receptionist who is joyful, cheerful, uplifting, encouraging, and positive can literally change the dynamic of your workplace.

In one organization where I worked, our job applicants were contacted via text messages and email to write anonymous reviews. This practice of soliciting reviews allowed us insight into the positive and negative experiences of our applicants while visiting our office. In one instance, we began receiving negative comments regarding one of the front desk team members. The applicant's comments cited the lack of a positive customer service experience. That situation was resolved quickly upon receipt of the applicant feedback. You can be sure that we took steps to ensure the atmosphere was changed.

Your front desk/reception person is just the tip of the iceberg. How about those that dedicate their day to face to face customer/client interaction as part of their responsibilities? You don't want your business representatives leaving a negative impression upon customers, clients, and prospects.  In addition to face to face customer/client interaction, think about those that spend their day on the phone with customers, clients, and prospects.  A few years back, while on a work conference call, one of my colleagues shared the following practice and principle with many in the organization.  The principle was that she had a note on her phone that said (paraphrased) "Am I smiling while on this phone call?"  It is amazing the difference detected in tone when someone is smiling while on the phone compared to the having a negative disposition.  It is more difficult to be mad, rude, or problematic with a smile on your face.

For this section of the interview, I like to ask candidates the question, "At the beginning of your workday, how do you interact with and greet your team or peers?"  I'm looking for any insight into how chipper the candidate is first thing in the morning.  I love, love, love walking into one of my offices and having team members greet me with a smile, a hearty "Good Morning," or a variety of other ways that demonstrate they are morning people.  In other not so glorious interactions, greetings can consist of, "Don't talk to me until my first cup of coffee!"

I recently read the book, *How Did You Do It Truett?*, by S. Truett Cathy.  I love the concept of having all team members respond to customers who say "thank you" with "my pleasure."  Those words exude superior customer service and are one of the many reasons why Chick Fil A is so successful.  If you haven't read this book by S. Truett Cathy I would highly encourage you to do so.

While candidates most certainly could try to pull the wool over your eyes by portraying themselves as cheerful when they really are not, there is a way to make this discovery.  Through the use of reference checks, you can ask their manager or supervisor, "Would you characterize (candidate) as joyful, cheerful, and happy?  Or, were they generally miserable, dissatisfied, and sad; being prone to mood swings?"

Another potentially important topic, in a similar vein of thought, could be the candidate's sense of humor. If a sense of humor is important for the position for which you are hiring you should absolutely ask if the candidate being interviewed believes that they have a sense of humor. Also, you can ask the candidate to describe their sense of humor for you. Of course, discerning if someone has a positive or negative sense of humor is important. You certainly don't want people on your team that have a crude, inappropriate, or vulgar sense of humor as that could expose your business or organization to allegations of harassment, mistreatment, or lack of mutual respect.

Ultimately, making sure that you hire a candidate that fits your expectations regarding outlook, countenance, and disposition is a critical step to ensure your organizational culture flourishes. If the Proverbial principle and concept of outlook, countenance, and disposition as it relates to being joyful is important to the position for which you are interviewing in your organization or business, I would suggest the usage of some of the potential interview questions listed below. The answers to these questions can help you make an assessment of your candidate's outlook, countenance, disposition, and joy.

- At the beginning of your workday, how do you interact with and greet your team or peers?

- When you think about your current or most recent job, what about it brought you joy, happiness, and cheer?

- When you think about your current or most recent job, what about it brought you misery, dissatisfaction, and sadness?

- When we ask your supervisor or manager this question, how will they respond? "Would you characterize (candidate) as joyful, cheerful, and happy or miserable, dissatisfied, and sad? Is the candidate prone to mood swings?"

- Do you have a sense of humor? Describe it.

# Chapter 3: INTELLIGENCE/QUEST FOR KNOWLEDGE, INSIGHT, AND WISDOM

Proverbs 15:14 The Message (MSG) **An intelligent person is always eager to take in more truth; fools feed on fast-food fads and fancies.**

Proverbs 2:1-2 The Message (MSG) **Good friend, take to heart what I'm telling you; collect my counsels and guard them with your life. Tune your ears to the world of Wisdom; set your heart on a life of Understanding.**

One of the areas of personal growth and improvement I have been working on is to become more of a reader. Although I'm not sure who to attribute the quote to, I've heard it said that leaders are readers...and I most certainly do believe the principle behind that saying. When I interview a candidate, I want to come to some determination if they have the potential to move up in the business or organization. Discovering someone's appetite toward personal growth by obtaining wisdom, insight, knowledge, and intelligence is important to determine if they have the drive to do more. While some positions I seek candidates for are purely entry level, I always want to try and develop the internal talent I have rather than seeking someone from outside the organization.

Inquiring about the candidate's personal development pattern through reading is important. I do want to make a note here that while reading physical books is important, I also utilize Audible heavily as I spend a lot of time on the road. This is a great way to take in information through long periods of windshield time.

A good way to make discovery about this topic during the interview is to ask questions about what the candidate is currently reading or studying, or what they have read or studied in the last several months. The answers to these questions are important, but what I really like to focus on is inquiring what the candidate has been able to apply from the reading or studying in either the personal or professional realm.

An additional question that might be helpful is to find out how the candidate best learns. Do they learn best from listening, watching, reading, or hands-on application? Through the interview process, you are looking for any areas of weakness in the candidate. Understanding how the candidate best learns can guide you into how to put together an action plan for these weaknesses if you hire the candidate. The action plan is for coaching and guiding the new hire to make any necessary improvements in order to have the highest opportunity for a successful placement.

Lastly, you could inquire what training sessions or seminars in which the candidate has recently participated. This could lead to a line of questioning which inquires what applications, takeaways, or improvements the candidate has made as a result of those training sessions or seminars.

One additional resource I would like to make note of is another of my books titled *Tips and Advice to Get a Job and Advance Your Career.*  This book is primarily geared toward entry level workers, and especially those entering the workforce upon transitioning from high school or college.  This book provides basic soft skills that many in the younger generation need to acquire in order to be successful in the work environment.  Additionally, the book gives the reader access to some of the countless reasons why thousands of employees are terminated from their places of employment and will help the reader gain valuable information as to why many applicants do not get job offers.  It will also help them gain a better understanding of what hiring professionals are looking for in job applicants.  All of this information will help them in their application, interview, and work endeavors for the rest of their life.

If you are struggling with soft skills improvements for anyone in your organization, providing *Tips and Advice to Get a Job and Advance Your Career* to them would be a great step for you to take in delivering the necessary information to make adjustments. Additionally, you should consider that book for all new employees you bring into the organization as an aid to ensure your expectations are rightly understood and able to be met.

*Tips and Advice to Get a Job and Advance Your Career* is available on Amazon at the following link.

http://amzn.com/B06XK7DPZ6

The following interview questions can help guide you into an assessment regarding this chapter's topic.

- Tell me what you are currently reading or studying.

- What else have you read or studied in the last 3 months?

- What have you been able to apply from the reading and/or studying personally and/or professionally?

- How do you best learn things?

- What training, seminars, etc. have you been through recently and how did that change you?

# Chapter 4: CONTENTMENT (PEACE)

Proverbs 15:16 The Message (MSG) **A simple life in the Fear-of-God is better than a rich life with a ton of headaches.**

Proverbs 12:20 The Message (MSG) **Evil scheming distorts the schemer; peace-planning brings joy to the planner.**

Matthew 5:9 New American Standard Bible (NASB) **Blessed are the peacemakers, for they shall be called sons of God.**

It is quite possible that a critical aspect of the decision-making process for the role you are interviewing and hiring for is to ensure you onboard someone who exhibits contentment and peace. As you look to build and grow an organization or business, having employees that fit your expected mold is important.

Unlike the last chapter, where we spoke about determining which of your candidates have the capacity or even forward-looking mindset to try and grow within your organization, there may be some positions where you simply want to hire someone into a spot where they may never have an opportunity for advancement. Historically, I can think back to many roles for which I've hired where it wasn't critical that the person have aspirations to move up in the organization. There will be positions that you just need someone to be faithful to crank out the work day in and day out in order to achieve your organizational objectives.

For these type of roles, you definitely want to make sure you get the best fit as with all positions in your business or organization. To get to the heart of the matter with the candidate, you could ask them about their goals, ambitions, and dreams. The answers to this question will give you insight into the candidate's mindset. Furthermore, you could ask the candidate how they go about determining or setting their goals. Understanding what influences they have in these areas will shed light on the determination if this candidate might be a good fit for the position. Additionally, you could inquire about what occupational or professional level, status, or position your candidate believes will bring them satisfaction, peace, and contentment.

While the aforementioned topics, questions, and resulting answers in this chapter can be important determining factors to obtain from the candidate, I believe this particular chapter's subject matter is another area where the reference check should come into play. Who better to give you an independent perspective about the engagement and satisfaction level of your candidate than their former supervisors or managers? Consider asking those supervisors or managers the following question, "Would you characterize the candidate as content, peaceful, and satisfied in their role? If so, explain why."

The following are some sample questions you can ask for this category.

- What are your goals, ambitions, and dreams?

- What occupational or professional level, status, or position will bring you satisfaction, peace, and contentment?

- When we ask your supervisor or manager this question, how will they respond? "Would you characterize (candidate) as content, peaceful, and satisfied in their role and why?"

- What is the process you go through to determine your goals?

# Chapter 5: CONFLICT AVOIDANCE AND RESOLUTION (SELF CONTROL)

Proverbs 15:18 The Message (MSG) **Hot tempers start fights; a calm, cool spirit keeps the peace.**

Thinking back through the years, I've definitely hired some employees that I later discovered were not adept at controlling their temper and/or working toward proper restoration or reconciliation once they had created a hostile situation. Also, I've inherited some employees through changing job duties, responsibilities, or markets where those employees exhibited the same kinds of issues. I can recall situations where those employees angered customers, clients, subordinates, peers, and leaders. The ability to hold their tongue and think through situations was not one of their strong suits. In client and customer incidents, I have quite literally seen and felt the negative consequences of greatly strained relationships until a resolution could be achieved.

My point in describing those situations is that you want to do everything you can to ensure you onboard candidates who are able to either avoid conflict or are able to tactfully, peacefully, and amicably bring situations they have created to a resolution. There are a couple of questions I use to try and uncover how the candidate deals with these types of situations. One effective line of questioning is to ask the candidate to describe their conflict avoidance and resolution skills, abilities, and concepts. Additionally, an extremely telling approach to take is to ask the candidate point blank to tell you about the last time they lost their temper at work and what was the resulting effect of that event.

However, even though these are direct questions about the topic, the candidate can attempt to side step or even not be factual about how they truly deal with those type of situations. Once again, I believe this is another area where the reference check should absolutely come into play. Who better to give you an independent perspective about their actual experiences with the candidate in the realm of conflict management than their former supervisors and managers? Asking those former supervisors and managers the following question should provide you some insight to make a good assessment into this category, "Would you characterize the candidate as peaceable and able to reconcile with others?"

Here are the potential interview questions you can ask as it relates to this chapter's content:

- Describe your conflict avoidance and resolution skills, abilities, and concepts.

- Tell me about the last time you lost your temper at work and what conflict or situation that caused.

- When we ask your supervisor or manager this question, how will they respond? "Would you characterize (candidate) as peaceable and able to reconcile with others and why?"

# Chapter 6: DILIGENCE AND EXCELLENCE (FAITHFULNESS)

Proverbs 15:19 The Message (MSG) **The path of lazy people is overgrown with briers; the diligent walk down a smooth road.**

Proverbs 10:26 The Message (MSG) **A lazy employee will give you nothing but trouble; it's vinegar in the mouth, smoke in the eyes.**

Now we enter one of my favorite topics, that of working with diligence and excellence. Being faithful to provide your employer with your best efforts is an obligation that we all have. I'll provide a quick excerpt from Day 49 of my book, *The 100 Day Vocabulary Word Devotional*, available at http://amzn.com/B01NARVGW3

> "...if you are faithful to execute all the jobs, tasks, processes, and duties that you have been assigned (and do them with diligence, integrity, and excellence) then your employer will have no reason to

discipline or terminate you because you will be considered a trusted, valued member of the organization. This faithfulness, diligence, integrity, and excellence should pertain to 100% of your responsibilities, no matter how large or small. No matter if you are in an entry level position or the president of the company you have a mandate to faithfully execute during each and every minute of every day you are at work."

As you think about diving into this topic during the interview process, there are a few questions that can be asked to start revealing, from the candidate's perspective, how much diligence and excellence they really exhibit in the workplace. First, you can ask the candidate to describe their work habits and schedule. Ask them to describe a time recently when diligence, wisdom, or creativity were applied in saving time, money, resources, or effort in their job or company. Consider asking them at what pace or speed they work. Another area of interest is to find out if they tend to procrastinate in any areas.

However, as with the topic in the previous chapter, the candidate can most certainly provide less than factual information.  So, once again, I highly recommend inquiring of those former supervisors and managers with the following question which should provide you some insight to make a good assessment into this chapter's topic, "Would you characterize the candidate as diligent and demonstrating excellence, being faithful in their work responsibilities?"

The bottom line for this chapter is that you need to make every effort to ensure the candidate you select has it within them to provide your business or organization the diligence and excellence you deserve.  Please take every step you can to gain insight into these areas.  At the outset of this chapter, I provided Proverbs 10:26 as a reference and it states, "A lazy employee will give you nothing but trouble."  Don't let trouble enter into your business or organization.

Here are some interview questions you can ask for this topic.

- Describe your work habits and schedule.

- Describe a time recently when diligence, wisdom, or creativity were applied in saving time, money, resources, or effort in your job or company.

- When we ask your supervisor or manager this question, how will they respond? "Would you characterize (candidate) as diligent and demonstrating excellence, being faithful in their work responsibilities, and why?"

- At what speed would you say you work?

- For what things do you procrastinate?

# Chapter 7: TIMING, CONTRIBUTION, AND CONTROL

Proverbs 15:23 The Message (MSG) **Congenial conversation—what a pleasure! The right word at the right time—beautiful!**

Proverbs 10:19 The Message (MSG) **The more talk, the less truth; the wise measure their words.**

Talking too much, talking too little...is there a perfect balance? For each position for which you are recruiting you'll need to determine if there is a level of talkativeness, or lack thereof, that meets your expectations. Or, is it even important at all to determine the level of talkativeness of the candidate? Are you willing to accept someone who is a continual chatterbox? Are you willing to accept someone that has a low level of verbal interaction with others but grinds out the work?

In addition to deciding about the level of talkativeness that you expect, you may also want to make a candidate assessment about the appropriateness of the verbal interaction, discussions, and responses to your questions. It isn't just about having the right mix or balance of words, but as Proverbs 15:23 says, using "the right word at the right time." Sometimes carrying on a conversational interview with a candidate can reveal troubling tendencies such as choppy or short responses, awkwardness, or difficult transitions.

This can be especially important as you consider the task of bringing sales professionals into your organization. You certainly don't want a sales person who talks excessively and who lacks the ability to question prospective customers, really listening to what they say. That characteristic will not allow the candidate to properly determine and assess what the prospect's true needs are, let alone brainstorm potential solutions.

Additional questions that you could ask in the interview to provide further clues about your candidate are as follows:

- When in a meeting, group think, or conversation what are your thoughts on how much you should participate?

- In your last meeting, conversation, or group think how much did you participate?

- Describe the last time you said the right thing at the right time and it changed the course of the meeting and ultimately the outcome or decision-making process.

- Have you ever had to conduct or lead meetings?

- What is the most troublesome aspect of conducting or leading meetings for you?

- When we ask your supervisor or manager this question, how will they respond? "How would you characterize (candidates) level of talkativeness? How would you characterize their ability to carry on a conversation that lacks awkwardness? (If appropriate) How would you describe their ability to appropriately balance speaking and listening during sales calls, presentations, or discovery sessions?"

The bottom line for this section is to ensure that your expectations are met in terms of the level of verbal interaction that the candidate you are considering possesses.

# Chapter 8: THOUGHTFULNESS (PATIENCE)

Proverbs 15:24 The Message (MSG) **Life ascends to the heights for the thoughtful—it's a clean about-face from descent into hell.**

Proverbs 25:15 The Message (MSG) **Patient persistence pierces through indifference; gentle speech breaks down rigid defenses.**

Regarding the position that you are recruiting for, how important is it that the candidate be thoughtful and patient? Is the position one where it's simply repetition, doing the same processes day in and day out with little need for variation, strategy, or planning? Or, is the position one where you definitely need someone to be thoughtful regarding the development of processes, ideas, strategies, and plans? How important is it in this position that the chosen candidate have patience to deal with difficult situations or people? These questions need to be resolved prior to entering the interview process in order to have an effective plan for making a determination.

If any of these topics are important, consider asking the following questions to come to a determination about the adequacy of the candidate being interviewed.

- Describe your habits as it pertains to dealing with issues or people; how patient are you to be thoughtful, reflective, and purposeful to plan, strategize, and execute on resolution?

- When we ask your supervisor or manager this question, how will they respond? "Would you characterize (candidate) as patient, thoughtful, planning, reflective, strategic, and visionary and why?"

# Chapter 9: ARROGANCE ABOUT BEING WRONG

Proverbs 15:25 The Message (MSG) **God smashes the pretensions of the arrogant; he stands with those who have no standing.**

Proverbs 28:13 The Message (MSG) **You can't whitewash your sins and get by with it; you find mercy by admitting and leaving them.**

How important is it that the candidate be willing to admit when they are wrong, have sinned against someone, offended someone, or are at fault for some reason? I've seen different internal, political, and relational dynamics within a multitude of businesses and organizations. Some have a culture where openness to the admission of wrongs, faults, or offense is 100% normal; however, for others the saying "throwing someone under the bus" comes to mind and is a regular and routine part of their daily practices.

I hope your business or organization adheres to the principles of being able to openly and honestly deal with situations that arise. Understanding if the candidate you are interviewing aligns with the dynamic within your organization can be a critical one. Consider the following possible questions to get a sense of where your candidate is on the spectrum of being able to resolve wrongdoing, offense, or faults.

- Provide the account of the last time you were wrong and how you dealt with it. What was the ultimate outcome of the situation?

- What are your expectations when dealing with errors, being wrong, or failing at a task?

- When a client or colleague is given bad, incorrect, or false information, how do you respond, recover, and rectify?

- Describe the last situation where you had to say "I'm sorry" to someone.

# Chapter 10: RECONCILIATION (KINDNESS)

Proverbs 15:26 The Message (MSG) **God can't stand evil scheming, but he puts words of grace and beauty on display.**

For this characteristic, we are looking at the flip side of what we discussed in Chapter 5: Conflict Avoidance and Resolution (Self-Control). In chapter 5, we sought information to lead us to an understanding if the candidate was someone who creates conflict, can't control their temper, and lacks peace as it pertains to personal interaction. For this chapter/topic, we are trying to discover whether the candidate is able to handle offense (rather than creating offense as in Chapter 5) in an appropriate manner.

In the work setting, as well as in our personal lives, it's important to make sure we are able to "play nicely in the sandbox", as the old saying goes. I believe this is one of the areas that you can't overlook in the interview process. While some of the other chapters/topics I present in this book could potentially be excluded in your specific interview process, understanding how someone interacts with others when the "heat is on", so to speak, is critically important. Allowing a candidate who is unable to handle offense in an appropriate manner to join your team can certainly open you up to significant problems down the road. Not only is handling the specific offensive incident, exchange, or situation important, but coming to an understanding of how the candidate is able to reconcile and work going forward with those who created the original offense is equally important.

As our Proverb in this chapter reveals, "words of grace and beauty" are the key element you are looking for in this characteristic. Is your candidate someone who can gracefully and kindly navigate the rough waters as it pertains to being on the receiving end of offense, disappointment, or anger? On the opposite end of the "words of grace and beauty" section of this Proverb, we see "God can't stand evil scheming." Is your candidate someone who would rather take the dramatic situation they've been pulled into and "share" the drama with other people, thus infecting other people's opinions of the person who allegedly created the offense? Is your candidate someone who "holds" the offense, disappointment, or anger for extended periods of time and is unable to ever truly deal with the root cause of the situation? Is your candidate someone who constantly wants to talk to others about the incident, exchange, or situation; but never wants to speak directly to the other party for the purpose of reconciliation and healing?

Below you will find some potential interview questions that you can use for this topic in your discovery process with the candidate.

- Describe how you reacted the last time someone offended you, disappointed you, or made you mad.

- How were you able to heal the relationship for the account you just provided?

- What are acceptable ways of dealing with people who offend you, disappoint you, or make you mad/angry?

- What rating would you give yourself, in terms of reacting kindly, when dealing with situations where you have been offended?

# **Chapter 11:** GREED AND ETHICS (GOODNESS)

Proverbs 15:27 The Message (MSG) **A greedy and grasping person destroys community; those who refuse to exploit live and let live.**

One particular owner of a business where I was employed was known for saying that all employees should always do the "right thing." Granted, the "right thing" is subject to interpretation or opinion and can mean different things to a variety of people. However, our Proverb for this chapter uses the word "exploit" and it certainly contains a negative connotation. I definitely want to know if the person I am considering hiring is someone who is not greedy, has an ethical or moral compass, and is genuinely a "good" person who always tries to do the "right thing."

While at first glance, the proposed, potential interview questions at the end of this chapter could appear to only pertain to those employed in a sales or customer service role, I believe there are implications and applications for those involved in almost any role in your business or organization. These interview questions can be tweaked for other processes, tasks, roles, or responsibilities in your business or organization. Consider the following concerns you could have about those in your organization that are not tied to sales or customer service. Are they willing to do anything and everything possible to:

- Get their "way"
- Get another position they want
- Get someone in the organization in trouble (i.e. "throw them under the bus", as my southern friends say)

However, for those in the sales or customer service arenas, the candidate's answers to the interview questions below will help provide insight into the candidate's mindset regarding how they deal with prospects, clients, customers, and business in general. What I've personally discovered in the sales and customer service arenas is that it is a battle in the marketplace to turn prospects into clients or customers.  It can be very difficult in certain market segments to gain new clients or customers, so the thought of losing a client or customer causes me much grief and pain because I know replacing that business could be problematic.  As such, ensuring your sales and customer service employees take great care to treat well what they have been entrusted with is critical.

- What was the last out of the box idea you employed to gain a client, customer, sale, or retain a client?

- What are unacceptable and acceptable methods of gaining business, customers, or sales?

- What is more important, gaining new clients, sales, business at any cost, or following a strict set of methods?

- Describe the word integrity. How have you had to bend or buckle as it pertains to your integrity?

# Chapter 12: CONTEMPLATION FOR THE RIGHT ANSWER

Proverbs 15:28 The Message (MSG) **Prayerful answers come from God-loyal people; the wicked are sewers of abuse.**

For this section/chapter, I absolutely understand that we can't ask questions in an interview about a candidate's religious, spiritual, prayer, or Bible opinions, outlook, or thoughts. However, you can ask questions that may give you some insight into, as this chapters Proverb says, "prayerful answers." The NASB version, for Proverbs 15:28 says "The heart of the righteous ponders how to answer." The bottom line for me is that I want to understand what the candidate's inclination is toward how they seek out, ponder, and obtain answers to difficult or problematic situations. While a candidate may not come right out and say they pray in order to find those answers (and I'm certainly not going to ask that question), they may share with you a more general process that they follow in contemplation for obtaining the right answer.

For this chapter or topic, my fear is that I will hire someone who snaps off answers without being reflective and thoughtful, thus potentially not providing the right answer. I also want to make sure that the candidate can wade through the waters of deferring to provide an answer and do so in a tactful manner. Are they prone to upsetting the apple cart in this process, thus leaving their boss, co-workers, customers, or clients feeling offended, disappointed, or mad? Are they able to deliver in these situations in such a way that they leave people feeling like they have received superior service in spite of not receiving an answer immediately?

The following questions are a good starting point to having the candidate reveal their tendencies.

- Tell about the last time you purposefully didn't answer a question (i.e. deferred in responding) to determine the right answer.

- How did you arrive at the right answer and how long did it take?

- Did anyone get offended, disappointed, or mad during the process of you deciding or responding?

- How do you go about analyzing difficult situations, issues, or decisions?

# Chapter 13: GOOD NEWS AND BAD NEWS; WINNING AND LOSING

Proverbs 15:30 The Message (MSG) **A twinkle in the eye means joy in the heart, and good news makes you feel fit as a fiddle.**

I do not like to lose…at anything! However, through the years, I've become very good at masking my frustration and disappointment when I lose. My competitive spirit rises up regardless if we are playing a family game of cards or on the basketball court with a group of guys competing fiercely. When losing a game some have falsely accused me of throwing the game so the other person could win. My wife and children will tell you that if you beat me, you earned it, because I will give it my all to win at anything and everything. My point to this insight into my personal psyche is that I am a good winner and I am a good loser. I do not taunt people when I win and I don't cry and whine when I lose. In the workplace there are times that the candidate you hire will win and lose at things pertaining to work. I want to know how they are going to handle the winning, losing, good news, bad news scenarios.

Words and phrases like gloating, mocking, taunting, throwing things in people's faces, lording it over them, etc. are not the things you want to hear come from the person you are interviewing. Additionally, you really don't want to hear those words or phrases come from their former managers or supervisors. This is another area where I would encourage you to seek out answers from former managers or supervisors on reference checks.

We spoke in an earlier chapter about the "atmosphere" of your physical place of employment being affected by the people in your organization as it pertains to their outlook, countenance, and disposition. The discussion in this chapter ties into that topic as well. The atmosphere can and will be affected by how someone receives good news and bad news as well as how employees win and lose. As an illustration of this, please consider the following.

At the time of writing of this book, I have lived in 3 states (Illinois, Missouri, and Alabama). For the state of Alabama, there is one day of the year that brings more division, strife, competition, and rivalry than any other. That day is a Saturday in November when Alabama and Auburn play their rivalry college football game known as the Iron Bowl. It's amazing how the atmosphere can change from one business or organization to another based on the outcome of one football game. How people receive good news and bad news as well as how they win or lose is extremely impactful.

- How did you respond, react, or communicate the last time you received good news?

- When you win at something, how do you celebrate?

- How did you respond, react, or communicate the last time you received bad news?

- When you lose at something, how do you cope, communicate, and overcome?

- What words will your supervisor/manager use to describe you when you win or receive good news?

- What words will your supervisor/manager use to describe you when you lose or receive bad news?

# Chapter 14: RECEIVING CORRECTION, ADVICE, COACHING, AND REPROOF

> Proverbs 15:31-32 The Message (MSG) **31 Listen to good advice if you want to live well, an honored guest among wise men and women. 32 An undisciplined, self-willed life is puny; an obedient, God-willed life is spacious.**

Shifting blame, denial, anger, attitude, and diversion are not words you want to have associated with the selected candidate you are hiring as it pertains to their ability to receive correction, advice, coaching, reproof, or mentoring. In a training program I went through many years ago, the organization providing the training declared that they wanted FAT people in their organization. In their context FAT had nothing to do with the candidate's body mass index or size, but was an acronym for the type of person they were looking for:

**F** Faithful
**A** Available
**T** Teachable

Although you would like your selected candidate to have all three characteristics, as it relates to this acronym and this chapter specifically, you definitely want your chosen candidate to be someone that exhibits the "T" in FAT as teachable. No matter what station, position, or role we presently hold, there isn't anyone who knows everything; we should all be in a position where we are willing and able to receive whatever correction, advice, coaching, reproof, and mentoring is necessary for us to grow in the business or organization where we are serving.

While it's never fun to have something pointed out to us that we are doing wrong, where we can make improvements, or just simply where we need to step it up, you don't want anyone in your business or organization who cannot receive instructive messages without a positive outlook. Therefore, for the wisdom in this chapter's

Proverb, please find below some questions that you can ask your candidate in order to determine where you might rate them in terms of receiving instruction.

- Tell about the last time your manager or supervisor gave you advice, reproof, correction, coaching, or mentoring.

- How did you receive that message? What frame of mind or attitude did it put you in?

- What did you do in reaction to that message?

- What will your manager or supervisor tell us about how you receive advice, reproof, correction, coaching, or mentoring (what words will they use to explain or describe you in this category)?

# Chapter 15: HUMILITY

Proverbs 15:33 The Message (MSG) **Fear-of-God is a school in skilled living—first you learn humility, then you experience glory.**

Proverbs 18:12 The Message (MSG) **Pride first, then the crash, but humility is precursor to honor.**

Let's focus for a moment on the positive aspects of what our two Proverbs in this chapter say about humility. In Proverbs 15:33 we see glory associated with humility and in Proverbs 18:12 we see honor associated with humility. Wouldn't it be great to have a business or organization full of employees who are empty of pride and full of humility, thus resulting in glory and honor saturating your business or organization? We are not referencing the type of glory and honor that are self-promoted but, rather, glory and honor that are heaped upon your employee as a result of a correct self-image while not seeking accolades for themselves. Think about the type of worker you want to have; Proverbs 22:29 gives us a little more insight into those that are just good at their work.

> (MSG) **Observe people who are good at their work—skilled workers are always in demand and admired; they don't take a backseat to anyone.**

At the end of the day, you are looking for workers that exhibit great skills and don't try to shine the spotlight on themselves. Rather, they receive admiration in their roles from others without solicitation. These are the type of employees who are in demand, can be trusted with much, and are promotable into higher level positions you might have open in the future.

Consider some of the questions listed below to make an assessment of your candidate's view of themselves and ability to exhibit humility. The last two questions might seem like they don't fit in this category. However, they are positioned in this section to help you discover how the candidate stands up to difficult deadlines in hopes that they will share how they handled themselves when they missed a cutoff or deadline.

- When was the last time you had to humble yourself and what was the situation?

- What was the outcome of that humility?

- What did you learn from that situation and how have you applied it?

- Describe the last situation where you did not meet a mandated deadline.

- How many times have you missed a deadline in your last role and over what time period?

# Chapter 16: LANGUAGE

Proverbs 10:31 The Message (MSG) **A good person's mouth is a clear fountain of wisdom; a foul mouth is a stagnant swamp.**

Proverbs 19:1 New American Standard Bible (NASB) **Better is a poor man who walks in his integrity than he who is perverse in speech and is a fool.**

This particular topic is one for which I take great personal interest. I do not like to hire people that I believe may cause issues, conflict, or strife with my clients, customers, internal team members, or anyone else based on the type of language that they use. I've seen situations where employees use foul, nasty, and perverse speech and it's caused relational issues both inside and outside the organizations where I have served.

I don't even want to take a chance on someone that has the bent toward using this type of language.  Relationships, serving clients/customers with excellence, and office interactions are hard enough to navigate and negotiate without throwing the foul language topic into the mix.  I steer clear of candidates if I detect that they have a propensity toward using this type of language.  Look at Proverbs 10:31 as quoted above…"a foul mouth is a stagnant swamp."  The word stagnant has the connotation of being stale and not fostering much in the way of positive momentum.  I don't want to align myself with employees whose mouths will result in negative consequences.

   Following you will find some interview questions that can help guide you into an understanding of where your candidate lands on the language spectrum.  This is another good topic to ask those with whom you will later be doing reference checks.

- When we ask your supervisor or manager this question, how will they respond? "Was (candidate) someone who used foul words/expressions, obscenities, or offensive language?"

- How do you feel about the use of foul or offensive language, coarse joking, or obscenities in the workplace?

- How has that type of language gotten you into negative workplace issues in the past?

# Chapter 17: THE TRUTH AND ETHICS

Proverbs 19:5 New American Standard Bible (NASB) **A false witness will not go unpunished, and he who tells lies will not escape.**

Proverbs 21:6 The Message (MSG) **Make it to the top by lying and cheating; get paid with smoke and a promotion—to death!**

Proverbs 10:9 The Message (MSG) **Honesty lives confident and carefree, but Shifty is sure to be exposed.**

Proverbs 10:18 The Message (MSG) **Liars secretly hoard hatred; fools openly spread slander.**

Much like the topic in the previous chapter regarding use of language, if I can determine that someone has a propensity toward lying, falsification, bending the truth, or whatever terminology you prefer to use; I will not hire them.  As those that know me in the work world will testify, one of my favorite words is transparency.  I would rather deal with a difficult situation up front with a client, employee, or someone to whom I report.  Trying to massage the situation to obtain an outcome that is somewhat shady, unethical, or wrong is not an option for me.  I learned a long time ago that honesty is the best policy.  If people can't trust you to tell the truth, why should they deal with you at all?  There is a saying that once was used frequently and goes as follows; "My Word is My Bond."  This saying simply means that you will do what you say, follow through, and not deceive people.  It can further be illustrated by the long lost art and practice of doing business by a handshake rather than with lengthy contracts.

At the end of the interview process, you really want to come to grips with the question, "Is this candidate trustworthy to tell the truth?"  If not, I would suggest that you pass on the candidate.  I've found great peace in my life by telling the truth.  I never have to worry about what I've previously said matching up with what is being said in the present. It's just as one of the Scriptures I referenced in the beginning of this chapter says; Proverbs 10:9 The Message (MSG) **Honesty lives confident and carefree.** I don't have to second guess myself. You want people working for you in whom you can have extreme confidence.

Below you will find some interview questions that can help guide you into an understanding of how trustworthy and honest your candidate really is. I highly recommend investigating this topic with those whom you will later be doing reference checks.

- When we ask your supervisor or manager this question, how will they respond? "Did you ever catch (candidate) in a lie, or multiple lies?"

- Do you tell lies?

- In what ways is it OK to bend the truth?

- How has telling lies gotten you into trouble in the past?

- Describe an ethical dilemma you faced, how you dealt with it, and what the result was.

# Chapter 18: GOSSIP

Proverbs 20:19 The Message (MSG) **Gossips can't keep secrets, so never confide in blabbermouths.**

Proverbs 29:12 The Message (MSG) **When a leader listens to malicious gossip, all the workers get infected with evil.**

I don't utilize "third person" language in conversation much at all. But, my leadership team members, when speaking about the teams that they lead, know the saying well, "Alan doesn't do drama." While every situation needs to be fully investigated to find out the truth of the matter, generally speaking, I've found the saying "Where there's smoke, there's fire" to be true. Many times there is a central player in "Dramaland" and there are multiple people that have issues with that central player.

I do not play with those that tend to create drama, stir the pot, and infect the rest of the team. I let my leaders know that if they can't get the central player to cease from that type of activity through coaching, counseling, or corrective action that we will make quick work of terminating the employment relationship for the central player. We spoke in an earlier chapter about the atmosphere of an organization. One sure way to establish a negative atmosphere in a business or organization is to allow dissension to run rampant. This type of activity causes a lack of harmony, decreased production, low morale, and a host of other negative outcomes.

Below you will find some interview questions to consider asking if this particular area is important to you.

- How has talking about others behind their backs gotten you into trouble?

- What is your outlook on office drama? Do you participate in it? How do you deal with it?

- Describe the last situation where you continually complained about difficulties, obstacles, situations, or people.

# Chapter 19: TEMPER (GENTLENESS)

Proverbs 20:2 The Message (MSG) **Quick-tempered leaders are like mad dogs—cross them and they bite your head off.**

Matthew 5:5 New American Standard Bible (NASB) **Blessed are the gentle, for they shall inherit the earth.**

On the very day that I'm drafting this chapter I had a Branch Manager contact me stating that one of our client's management team members had yelled at one of our branch team members for making an inquiry into a situation that needed resolution. Unbeknownst to me, this was the second time this same client management team member had "bitten the head off" one of my branch team members. At this point, my intervention will be required to gingerly handle the topic. The Branch Manager believes that this client management team member has the reputation, even among the client's employees, of being a hothead.

While I understand that there are certainly situations or events in business that cause stress, there really isn't a reason for anyone to holler, scream, yell, cuss out, bite your head off, or in general verbally berate another person. All situations can be handled in a calm, cool, and gentle manner. If you allow (either directly with permission or indirectly by not dealing with the matter) a person in your business or organization to treat colleagues, clients, or customers with this type of negative attitude, you are hamstringing your business or organization. I don't like dealing with difficult people and I'm fairly confident most people don't either. However, we must deal with these types of people immediately. As it pertains to the discovery process during interviews, you need to come to some insight as to how the candidate you are interviewing handles stress and difficult situations. It's amazing when you phrase questions the right way how people will answer. With regard to the third question listed below, I've literally had people express to me very problematic situations that have helped me to make a quick decision as to the candidate's future with the business where I am employed.

You will find below some questions that you can consider asking if finding someone gentle, rather than given to fits of temper, is critically important for the position you are looking to fill.

- When have others described you as a hothead?

- How are you able to control your temper, anger, and words?

- When was the last time you lost it and reacted in angry manner where you later regretted it?

# Chapter 20: THE BEST IN QUALITY AND SERVICE

Proverbs 20:8-9 The Message (MSG) **Leaders who know their business and care keep a sharp eye out for the shoddy and cheap, for who among us can be trusted to be always diligent and honest?**

In Proverbs 20:8-9, the emphasis is on poor quality or inferior products. In addition to products that are poor or inferior, I also want to ensure that we take into account the service industry as well. It's not just products that can be poor or inferior. Service levels can be poor or inferior. Consider how words like excellence, high quality, and superior should factor into what we are producing or providing. The Proverb referenced above is specifically speaking about leaders and how they manage, oversee, or lead the efforts of their business or organization. Ultimately, all does roll up to the leader and the leader is responsible for everything that occurs in the business or organization. In order for a leader to ensure the highest opportunity for success, he or she must have systems in place to only bring in the highest caliber employees who will fulfill the expectations, goals, vision, and plans of the business or organization's leader.

Trying to recruit, attract, and onboard candidates that have a track record in their current or past roles of trying to make products or services better is one way to take steps toward providing the highest opportunity for success in your business or organization. While it would certainly be great to have highly creative employees who can develop their own ways to make products or services better, at a minimum, a candidate should have a system to discover, discern, and apply the best practices that have been developed by others. That is why question number 4 listed below is in this section of possible interview topics. Question number 4 is really an extension of what we discussed in chapter 3 regarding a candidate's quest for knowledge, insight, and wisdom. It is important to find out real examples of what candidates have mined out and implemented in current or past roles.

Consider the following interview questions as you try to come to an understanding of your candidate's propensity toward quality in products or services.

- When we say the words excellence, quality, and exceptional regarding work, quality, and service what comes to your mind?

- What lessons have you learned about things that are cheap and shoddy?

- How do you keep an eye out to ensure shoddiness and cheapness don't creep into any areas of work?

- How have you applied best practices or taken from what others have perfected to apply it to your processes, systems, products, services, etc?

# Chapter 21: BALANCE

Proverbs 21:17 The Message (MSG) **You're addicted to thrills? What an empty life! The pursuit of pleasure is never satisfied.**

Ecclesiastes 4:7-12 The Message (MSG) **7-8 I turned my head and saw yet another wisp of smoke on its way to nothingness: a solitary person, completely alone—no children, no family, no friends—yet working obsessively late into the night, compulsively greedy for more and more, never bothering to ask, "Why am I working like a dog, never having any fun? And who cares?" More smoke. A bad business. 9-10 It's better to have a partner than go it alone. Share the work, share the wealth. And if one falls down, the other helps, but if there's no one to help, tough! 11 Two in a bed warm each other. Alone, you shiver all night. 12 By yourself you're unprotected. With a friend you can face the worst. Can you round up a third? A three-stranded rope isn't easily snapped.**

For this section on balance, I've pulled in some of Solomon's wisdom outside the book of Proverbs as found in the book of Ecclesiastes. As you consider and contrast the listed verse from Proverbs and verses from Ecclesiastes, you'll see that there needs to be a balance between work and pleasure. In the verse from Proverbs, a total abandonment toward pleasure and thrills is spoken against. In thinking through the history of my life there have been times when a certain amusement, entertainment, or sport has taken the position of extreme prominence. While it may not have taken the focus off my occupational responsibilities, it certainly took away from my responsibilities toward Kingdom focused activities. I can cite instances of people I'm associated with that have gotten this area of their life out of balance and it has caused significant negative issues.

On the other hand, as we look at the verse in Ecclesiastes, an imbalance focused on extremism regarding work, occupation, and the gathering of money is also improperly aligned with God's intentions and best for people. During the interview process you can attempt to gain some insight into your candidate's history as it pertains to balancing work and life by asking a few questions. While you certainly can't pry into areas of the candidate's life that would be considered illegal or potentially discriminatory, some general questions can lead to insight important for you to gather. Below, I've listed some potential interview questions to assist you in the process to see if there is an imbalance one way or the other.

One last item to consider for this chapter or area is that, as a leader in your business or organization, you set the example for this particular topic. If you, or other influential members of your business or organization, have an imbalance toward either work or life, that speaks volumes to those who are being led. Regardless of what you might verbally say about work-life balance, what you do speaks louder. Do you need to make a change in this area of your life?

- Describe the current level of balance in your work life.

- What are areas that you need to work on to ensure a proper work balance?

- What would cause you distraction as it pertains to the focus you can allocate to work?

- Would you consider yourself a risk-taker or risk-avoider? Describe your level, depth, and capacity for risk taking or risk avoidance.

# Chapter 22: REPUTATION

Proverbs 22:1 The Message (MSG) **A sterling reputation is better than striking it rich; a gracious spirit is better than money in the bank.**

Maybe you've heard the phrase "Your reputation precedes you?" This phrase and identification can be used with either a positive or negative outlook depending on the context. In the Proverb listed for this chapter, Proverbs 22:1, having a sterling or positive reputation is absolutely the goal. During the interview and discovery process you certainly want to use diligence to reveal the perceived "reputation" of your candidate. I use the word perceived, because perception and reality aren't always aligned. You need to be as thorough as possible in order to make a determination about what is accurate.

Bringing someone onto your team that has a bad reputation can cause a ripple effect in your business or organization. While you should ask questions of the candidate during the interview about how the candidate believes that they are perceived in terms of reputation, that is only one perspective on the matter. Do your homework in order to discover the reality of the matter. I am defining doing your homework as performing the reference checks that we've been discussing throughout many of the preceding chapters. In addition, if legal where you operate your business or organization, criminal background checks are a very good way to discover the reality of the matter. Please consult your human resources professional or legal counsel on the matter of criminal background checks.

You will find below a few questions to consider during the interview process.

- When we speak to former managers, supervisors, co-worker and/or subordinates, what words will they use when asked to describe your "reputation"?

- When we ask those same people to rate you on being kind, gentle, merciful, peaceable, and self-controlled, what will they say?

- What are areas that you need to work on to promote a better "reputation"?

- What are the areas of your life that, if you could, you would go back to prevent "reputation" damage?

# Chapter 23: ASSOCIATIONS

Proverbs 22:11 The Message (MSG) **God loves the pure-hearted and well-spoken; good leaders also delight in their friendship.**

Proverbs 22:24-25 The Message (MSG) **Don't hang out with angry people; don't keep company with hotheads. Bad temper is contagious—don't get infected.**

Maybe you've heard of the old saying/proverb that goes like this, "Birds of a feather flock together." If you have not heard of this saying/proverb, it basically refers to people that have similar interests, mindsets, ideals, characteristics, or backgrounds that tend to group, identify, or hang out with each other. In some circles this might be referred to as a "clique" that can be exclusive, thus not allowing others into the group.

The point to providing this saying/proverb in this section is to help you understand that for screening, interviewing, and hiring purposes it might not be a bad idea to try to find out a little bit about your candidate's circle of influence. The first three proposed interview questions listed below are an attempt to try and gain some sort of understanding of the circles in which your candidate runs. By asking questions about your candidate's friends, co-workers, and those with whom they regularly associate, you can potentially open a window into your candidate's mindset.

The last question listed below is a derivation of the first three questions in that, with this question, you are attempting to gain some understanding about your candidate's outlook, mindset, and history regarding trying to network. When thinking about the word networking, you can approach this question from several perspectives. Is the candidate a part of industry trade associations, groups, or societies? If so, at what level do they participate in those activities? What is the candidate's mindset toward connecting with new people (both inside and outside of their industry, occupation, or trade)?

How has your candidate enriched the lives of others with whom they have connected? Or, does your candidate seem to be one that only "takes" from those with whom they form associations or connections?

For this particular category, I believe it is important to make a determination if your candidate can help your organization to source candidates for other open positions you may be looking to fill.

- When you think about friends, co-workers, and those with whom you associate regularly, how would you describe them?

- What types of people do you like to associate with?

- How do those you associate with make your life better or worse?

- Describe how you network both personally and professionally.

# Chapter 24: CRISIS MANAGEMENT

Proverbs 24:10 The Message (MSG) **If you fall to pieces in a crisis, there wasn't much to you in the first place.**

In my personal experience, crisis situations are not something that can be avoided. When thinking about all the different dynamics of business, (clients, customers, employees, etc.) difficult situations and challenges just seem to happen. What is important to me personally, is how I handle these situations or challenges. Additionally, I want a team surrounding me that has the ability to handle these situations and challenges in an appropriate manner. As I contemplate this particular area of job candidate diagnostics, I can think back to many past examples of team members that either fell apart or stepped it up during difficult times.

During the interview process, I want to be able to gain a glimpse into the actual, real, and historical crisis management that the candidate has undertaken. By asking the first question at the end of this chapter, it doesn't give the candidate the option for thinking about a situation or challenge that may not have been extremely difficult. However, it places the candidate in the position of providing the details around the last crisis which they had to manage. I don't want to provide the candidate with a choice of selecting a crisis but I am making them discuss what happened most recently.

In addition, the third question listed below corners the candidate into providing information on a situation that they did not handle well. I want to look at how the candidate learns, recovers, and changes going forward based on a situation where they may have failed. Failure is something that we all have to deal with at one point or another, but the true test is how we exit the situation or crisis. I want to see if the candidate has the ability to follow the positive path forward as described in the book *Failing Forward* by John Maxwell. Or, is the candidate one who can't seem to recover and press forward in a positive manner upon failing?

- What was the last crisis that you had to deal with?

- What lessons have you learned from having to deal with crises?

- As you reflect, describe the last crisis that you didn't handle well and how it turned out?

# Chapter 25: RESPECTING AUTHORITY

Proverbs 24:21-22 The Message (MSG) **Fear God, dear child—respect your leaders; don't be defiant or mutinous. Without warning your life can turn upside down, and who knows how or when it might happen?**

John Cougar Mellencamp said it well in his 1983 "*Authority Song*" with the lyrics "I fight authority, authority always wins." For the Proverb selected in this section, as it pertains to the interviewing, screening, and hiring process, I want to obtain as much information as I can about the candidate's attitude and mindset toward leadership, authority, and the chain of command.

Making a determination about the candidate's propensity toward being respectful, compliant, and submissive to leadership and authority is critically important. However, please don't think that I only want to hire candidates who will be a doormat. There are situations where leaders do need to be confronted. When I use the word confront(ed), I mean bringing something to the attention of a leader. What I do not mean when using the word confront(ed) is someone who has a negative, offensive, or hostile attitude (being confrontational). There is definitely a way to confront people with situations or issues in a non-confrontational manner that results in a positive outcome.

By asking some, or all, of the suggested questions below, you may be able to get at the heart of the respect matter very quickly. Question #1 is an open-ended question that leaves the person being asked without the option of saying "Yes" or "No." The answer will either be to name the person and why they didn't respect them or to say that they have never had a respect issue with any of their leaders. However, once they answer with the name of a person they didn't respect, you can continue to ask follow up questions about that situation to see their attitude and mindset on how they, in actuality and reality, deal with these type of leaders. In addition, once given the first name and situation, it is fair game to ask which other leaders they have worked for that they held in little or no regard. You can keep diving as deep as necessary until you feel you have satisfactory responses.

At the end of this line of questioning, you simply want to have some clear understanding on if your candidate is someone that is going to potentially cause drama, create conflict, and generate issues in your business or organization.

- Which of your leaders did you hold little or no regard for, and why?

- How did you deal with those leaders?

- Describe a situation where you tried to oust one of your leaders and take their position.

- How do go about obeying a leader despite having respect issues for them?

- When we speak to former managers, leaders, and supervisors what words will they use to describe your respect for authority or leadership?

# Chapter 26: LISTENING

Proverbs 18:15 The Message (MSG) **Wise men and women are always learning, always listening for fresh insights.**

Remember the saying that I introduced in Chapter 1, regarding how well your candidate seeks advice from others and relies on those in their circle of influence for necessary information? The saying went like this...

*God gave us two ears and one mouth. We should listen twice as much as we speak.*

For this section, I want to introduce something that I use in business as well as in my personal interactions with others. The topic in question is that I love, love, love, to ask questions of people. It doesn't matter if it's a new client, someone I'm networking with, someone I've just met on a personal basis, etc., but I really like trying to find out about and understand what makes that person tick. This process allows me to easily implement the "We should listen twice as much as we speak" methodology. I find myself trying to not tell people who I am, what I am about, and what makes me tick, in order to find out more about them.

For me, this entire interview process, methodology, and model that I am writing about in this book helps me adhere to the saying "We should listen twice as much as we speak." By asking a lot of questions, I minimize the amount of time I (or the interview panel) talk during the interview. This maximizes the amount of time that the candidate is talking. My objective in this process is to find out as much as I can about the candidate in an effort to make the best hiring decision possible.

The suggested questions listed below will help you to gain some insight into the candidate's propensity toward being the center of attention or making others the center of attention. Think about how your candidate lines up with the following wisdom from Philippians 2:3-4.

**(NASB) 3 Do nothing from selfishness or empty conceit, but with humility of mind regard one another as more important than yourselves; 4 do not *merely* look out for your own personal interests, but also for the interests of others.**

- When in a conversation with either those in authority over you, peers, or those in a subordinate position, how would you describe your listening skills?

- How do you fully concentrate on what the other person is saying in order to understand them completely?

- When we do reference checks, how will those we inquire of describe your listening skills? Will they say you are someone who cuts other people off while they are speaking?

# Chapter 27: CUSTOMER/CLIENT SERVICE

Proverbs 11:25 The Message (MSG) **The one who blesses others is abundantly blessed; those who help others are helped.**

Superior customer service is something that I take very seriously. When I have staff members that do not demonstrate superior customer service, we quickly make attempts to redeem the staff member through coaching and counseling. Ultimately, if the team member cannot make the necessary changes to be compliant, we work toward terminating that employee and recruiting someone who can exhibit the required level of customer service. In chapter 2, I cited an instance where a front desk team member was creating a negative atmosphere in our office. This information was received through a series of responses to anonymous surveys conducted on those who had visited our office. That is how seriously we take customer service.

Prior to hiring someone, I want to understand how they view themselves in terms of customer service. By asking the proposed interview questions listed below you can gain the necessary insight into the candidate's disposition, mentality, and outlook towards how they will deal with your customers and clients. Does their disposition, mentality, and outlook line up with the values in your business or organization? Questions two and three proposed below will get you to the meat of the matter by having the candidate provide you real life information and instances of superior customer service.

I suppose this matter could be summed up by looking at what has been referred to in the Bible as the Golden Rule as stated in Matthew 7:12.

**(NASB) In everything, therefore, treat people the same way you want them to treat you.**

- Describe your customer or client service skills, mentality, and outlook.

- What was the last situation where you went above and beyond to ensure customer or client satisfaction was achieved?

- How many customers or clients have you lost in the last two years and why did you lose them?

# Chapter 28: COMMUNICATION SKILLS

Proverbs 1:1-6 The Message (MSG) **1-6 These are the wise sayings of Solomon, David's son, Israel's king—Written down so we'll know how to live well and right, to understand what life means and where it's going; A manual for living, for learning what's right and just and fair; To teach the inexperienced the ropes and give our young people a grasp on reality. There's something here also for seasoned men and women, still a thing or two for the experienced to learn—Fresh wisdom to probe and penetrate, the rhymes and reasons of wise men and women.**

Proverbs 12:14 The Message (MSG) **Well-spoken words bring satisfaction; well-done work has its own reward.**

The Proverbs listed above for this chapter contain a theme surrounding the ability to communicate well. In these Proverbs we see both verbal and written communication skills being highlighted.  It's vitally important to be able to speak well with clients, customers, vendors, and those within our own business or organization.  Proverbs 12:14 above further shares that it's not just the right words being uttered but the way in which they are conveyed or "well-spoken."

Additionally, it's important to be able to express yourself in written format as well as verbally.  Much of today's business communication is conducted via email.  One of the more embarrassing things for me is to find an error, misspelled words, or grammatical issue with one of my own emails.  I have also been embarrassed and frustrated by team member's construction of emails and related errors, misspelled words, or grammatical issues.  I definitely want all communication to be done at a highly professional level and I first and foremost hold myself to that standard.

The proposed interview questions below should provide you some insight into your candidate's strengths and weaknesses as it pertains to communication.

- Describe your communication skill/level, both spoken and written.

- What is your preferred method of communication?

- What are areas where you know you need to improve regarding communication?

- When we do reference checks with former supervisors, peers, and subordinates how will they describe your written and verbal communication skills?

# Chapter 29: FOSTERING TEAMWORK AND DEMONSTRATING (LOVE) FOR OTHERS

Proverbs 2:9-15 The Message (MSG) **So now you can pick out what's true and fair, find all the good trails! Lady Wisdom will be your close friend, and Brother Knowledge your pleasant companion. Good Sense will scout ahead for danger, Insight will keep an eye out for you. They'll keep you from making wrong turns or following the bad directions of those who are lost themselves and can't tell a trail from a tumbleweed, these losers who make a game of evil and throw parties to celebrate perversity, traveling paths that go nowhere, wandering in a maze of detours and dead ends.**

Proverbs 8:12 The Message (MSG) **I am Lady Wisdom, and I live next to Sanity; Knowledge and Discretion live just down the street.**

Proverbs 17:17 The Message (MSG) **Friends love through all kinds of weather, and families**

**stick together in all kinds of trouble.**

Proverbs 10:12 The Message (MSG) **Hatred starts fights, but love pulls a quilt over the bickering.**

For the first two Proverbs listed for this chapter (2:9-15 and 8:12), I would request that you re-read these prior to proceeding, please. As you read over these two Proverbs again, look for the names of the team members we should be selecting. Did you catch them? I see **<u>Lady Wisdom</u>**, **<u>Brother Knowledge</u>**, **<u>Good Sense</u>**, **<u>Insight</u>**, **<u>Sanity</u>**, and **<u>Discretion</u>** listed. If ever there was an All-Star team that was to be assembled, I would want each of these players on my squad.

Recently I did a teaching on Proverbs 9:1 (listed below in the NASB version):

> **Wisdom has built her house,**
> **She has hewn out her seven pillars.**

In that teaching I referenced Proverbs 8:12-14,

which is a potential answer to the seven pillars of Proverbs 9:1. Those supporting structures (pillars) that provide coverage, protection, and strength for the house are as follows in Proverbs 8:12-14:

- **prudence**
- **knowledge *and* discretion**.
- **fear of the Lord**
- **counsel**
- **sound wisdom**
- **understanding**
- **power**

As we think about all these attributes, characteristics, and mindsets they are all players that we want on our team. Additionally, we want our team to be harmonious. As you go through the interview process, I recommend using the proposed questions below to assess your candidate's ability to play well with these team members as well as to love their team members.

- When we do personal reference checks of your manager/supervisor, peers, and subordinates, what will they say in terms of rating you on fostering and partnering with others in teamwork?

- In many work situations, people spend more of their daily awake hours around those we work with rather than family or friends. It has been said that our co-workers can be like our second family. How would you describe the overall attitudes, thoughts, and feelings you have about your work family compared to your relational family and personal friends?

- Tell me about a time you helped, supported, loved, and encouraged someone at work who was going through a difficult period.

- Describe the last time you actively sought out someone in your work family that could help you make improvements, become a better person/worker, or help you to provide more value for your employer.

- Do you prefer to work individually or on a team and why?

# Chapter 30: THE ART OF CONVINCING THROUGH PATIENCE

Proverbs 25:15 The Message (MSG) **Patient persistence pierces through indifference; gentle speech breaks down rigid defenses.**

I would say that being someone who can be persuasive is important. However, there are limitations and boundaries to the type of methods that should be employed to persuade people. I've seen the methods of intimidation, coercion, and badgering used to convince or persuade people to perform jobs or tasks. I do not appreciate it when someone lowers themselves to these types of methods because they are unable to effectively state their case, in what our Proverb for this chapter outlines, in a gentle and patient way.

There is a saying that I've often quoted and used in various situations that says, "A man convinced against his will is of the same opinion still." Upon researching this saying or quotation there appears to be some disagreement as to who originally penned the words. I don't think it really matters who gets credit for the quote. The point is there are people who employ such methods to persuade, convince, or coerce others. Although they "get their way," the one who acquiesces may only do so in order to get the person off their back.

We've already talked about teamwork in a previous chapter, and this chapter's topic seems to be somewhat of an extension to the area of teamwork. The first three proposed questions below deal with attempts to understand how the candidate you are interviewing feels they interact with others in these types of situations. The fourth question proposed below is not necessarily in the same vein, however it is an important tangent in determining how your candidate relates to other people when faced with difficult, stressful, or controversial topics, people, or decisions. You will want to gain some insight into what, if any, areas you will need to train, provide, or mentor this candidate, if you make the decision to onboard them.

- Would you consider yourself someone who can convince or persuade others when necessary?

- If so, what methods do you employ to persuade or convince others?

- When we do personal reference checks of your manager/supervisor, peers, and subordinates what will they say about this category? Will they say you wear people down or work collectively to achieve the necessary results?

- What type or level of training or coaching do you need as it pertains to conflict management?

# Chapter 31: BRIDGING THE GAP

Proverbs 22:2 The Message (MSG) **The rich and the poor shake hands as equals—God made them both!**

Proverbs 29:14 The Message (MSG) **Leadership gains authority and respect when the voiceless poor are treated fairly.**

By now, due to my extensive citation of Proverbs, you may have detected that Proverbs is my favorite book of the Bible. It is so rich and full of wisdom that I love mining it out each day for applicability to my life. Next in my line of favorites in addition to the book of Proverbs is the book of James. James also holds much "get up in your grill" teaching that requires much introspection. As it pertains to this chapter I would like, in addition to the two Proverbs cited above, to provide a portion of James that ties right in with this chapter's theme.

James 2:1-4 The Message (MSG) **My dear**

**friends, don't let public opinion influence how you live out our glorious, Christ-originated faith. If a man enters your church wearing an expensive suit, and a street person wearing rags comes in right after him, and you say to the man in the suit, "Sit here, sir; this is the best seat in the house!" and either ignore the street person or say, "Better sit here in the back row," haven't you segregated God's children and proved that you are judges who can't be trusted?**

Now, let's get to it in terms of how we need to apply the Scriptures we've read in the Chapter to the screening and interviewing process. Just because you may think, detect, or assume that someone comes from a socio-economic status, situation, or group, this should not lead you to ignore, overlook, or shun them. God allocates gifts, skills, abilities, and talents liberally and you must look deep and hard to determine if what your applicant possesses meets the requirements that will best align or match to the position for which you are recruiting. First and foremost, you must look introspectively to determine if you have any biases that are undermining the selection process in terms of hiring the best candidate possible. Secondly, you should dig deep while interviewing candidates to determine if they have any biases, mindsets, or outlooks that will affect the team concept that you are trying to build in your business or organization.

I want to know, when interviewing candidates, if they cannot play well in the sandbox with individuals of other backgrounds, beliefs, or socio-economic status. The questions listed below are a few samples that I've used in the interview process to try to come to an assessment regarding how well the candidate is going to work with others that are different from them. Sometimes, during the interview, I've got to continue digging deeper, asking questions based on the answers given in the interview. Sometimes it's not the actual verbal responses given that clue me in to issues but the demeanor, expressions, pauses, or other non-verbal signals that cause me to continue probing until I am satisfied that I have been provided all the information I need to obtain.

This is another one of the categories where I highly recommend asking references what their thoughts are regarding how well the candidate in question works with individuals of different background, beliefs, or socio-economic status.

- What is your approach to working with people of different backgrounds, beliefs, or socio-economic status?

- Tell about a time where you were named in an allegation of not working well with, or treating unfairly, someone of a different background, belief, or socio-economic status.

- How have you fostered healing, restoration, or reconciliation in a situation as described above?

# Chapter 32: INITIAL REACTION

Proverbs 17:22 The Message (MSG) **A cheerful disposition is good for your health; gloom and doom leave you bone-tired.**

In the course of reading articles and books, as well as just generally observing how I and others assess people upon the initial introduction or meeting, it's become apparent to me that quick and hasty initial reactions, assessment, and judgments are made about people the first time we meet them. Sometimes those initial reactions, assessment, and judgments are proven wrong. However, sometimes they are proven to be spot on accurate.

During the interview process I like to try and determine what the candidate thinks are others' first impressions of them. This may seem like a very simple question, but I can't tell you the number of times that this question has been met by delayed responses. By delayed responses, I mean that the candidate has to really think about it for a while before answering. It may be that this is a question that many people honestly never consider, and it really throws them for a loop.

In chapter 2 we discussed the concept of outlook, countenance, and disposition. Proverb 17:22, as listed in the beginning of this chapter, ties right into the chapter 2 topic. However, in chapter 2, we approached the subject from an ongoing and daily personal interaction perspective rather than the subject of first impressions. As it pertains to first impressions, you need to assess how critical it is for the candidate you want to select to be able to make great first impressions. For many positions you are recruiting, screening, and interviewing for, it will be critical to ensure the selected candidate has the ability to give a good first impression. Some of these positions include sales, customer service, and reception, among other positions that may require this skill.

While there are only a couple of recommended interview questions listed below, they should provide you some valuable insight into how your candidates perceive that others assess them. Once again, if the topic of this chapter is a critical component for the selection process and you have some lack of direction or discernment on this topic, who better to get another perspective from that the references you will be calling?  Feel free to ask the references what their first impression was upon meeting the candidate.

- How do you think people react when they first meet you (i.e. what sort of impression do they have of you)?

- What do you need to change to become more likeable to others?

In these first 32 chapters we have dealt with topics that can be applicable to many positions you are recruiting, screening, and interviewing to fill.  From entry level to executive suite, the first 32 chapters are worthy of consideration into the interview process.  For the remainder of the book, we will look at some topics that deal specifically with supervisory, managerial, and leadership positions.  While there may be some nuggets you can pull out for other positions in your organization, I believe that you really need to focus your attention on the remaining chapters for the higher level positions in your business or organization.

# Chapter 33: TAKING ACTION WHEN NEEDED

Proverbs 24:11-12 The Message (MSG) **Rescue the perishing; don't hesitate to step in and help. If you say, "Hey, that's none of my business," will that get you off the hook? Someone is watching you closely, you know— Someone not impressed with weak excuses.**

While the context of this verse pertains to the "perishing," or those that are being mistreated for the purpose of their ultimate death, there certainly are parallels to lesser versions of negative behavior, treatment, or punishment as it pertains to the workplace. Through the course of many years in the field of Human Resources and in the Staffing industry, I've had to step into situations where physical altercations, verbal harassment, and general mistreatment were taking place. It's certainly not fun to have to deal with these situations, but in many of the roles and responsibilities that you may be recruiting, screening, and interviewing for, someone has to take charge and ensure that fairness, equity, and justice are the ultimate outcome.

This topic may not be important if you are interviewing for an entry level position in your organization, but I would submit that for supervisory, managerial, and leadership roles the selected candidate needs to be someone who has the confidence and ability to step into potentially volatile situations and navigate the path toward peace. In the current climate where many times it seems that anyone can initiate legal action for any type of crazy situation, you want to make sure you have leaders that can properly handle matters that could potentially lead to litigation.

Having said all that, if you deem this topic necessary for the position you are hoping to fill, you might want to consider the questions listed below. These questions can help determine if you are interviewing a candidate who will shrink back when difficult matters arise, or if the candidate gives you the confidence that they can handle problematic issues.

- Tell about the last time you had to step into a difficult situation to act, displaying assertiveness.

- Describe how you are assertive enough for the job for which you are interviewing for today.

# Chapter 34: DISCIPLINE AND TERMINATION

> Proverbs 20:26 The Message (MSG) **After careful scrutiny, a wise leader makes a clean sweep of rebels and dolts.**

Unfortunately, the territory of management and leadership comes with the charge of walking through the minefield of employee management. Few things rival the infection that can spread through a business or organization like an employee that can't follow processes, procedures, and policies or cannot perform to the organizational expectations. When these situations occur, the infectious behavior, attitudes, and actions tend to lower the morale of the rest of the team. As a manager or leader, you have the responsibility to deal with these situations promptly and thoroughly but with a healthy dose of grace and mercy in order to make all attempts to redeem the team member who is causing strife.

One of the least favorite aspects of my roles and responsibilities is that sometimes an employee needs to be separated from the business or organization. I mentioned in the acknowledgement section of this book that Neil Kennedy has taught me much. One of the things I've learned from his teachings is the concept that when we separate, terminate, or release someone (whatever you wish to call it), it is for the purpose of allowing that person to find their area of giftedness somewhere else in life. Just because they cannot be successful in your business or organization doesn't mean that they are incapable of contributing in some other role or responsibility at another business or organization. Even though we must make tough decisions about discipline and termination, we should frame those conversations around the idea of redemption, improvement, and finding a place to thrive within their gift and talent set.

As such, during the interview process for managers and leaders, I want to make inquiries aimed at finding out the applicant's mindset and philosophy surrounding discipline and termination. Furthermore, rather than just finding out their theories about discipline and termination, I want to discover what their past practices, applications, and experiences reveal about how the applicant has actually treated and handled past situations. While past performance may not be an indicator of future results, it's certainly one way to at least formulate some assessment. The questions listed below can begin the process of digging into these topics. I recommend you consider their usage in your interviewing process for managers and leaders.

- Describe the process you go through in determining if and when to discipline or terminate someone.

- What issues have you run into in the past regarding discipline or termination?

- If you could, what things would you change from the past regarding discipline or termination of others?

- How do you deal with underperforming team members?

# Chapter 35: LEADERSHIP TRAITS

> Proverbs 20:28 The Message (MSG) **Love and truth form a good leader; sound leadership is founded on loving integrity.**

In the previous chapter, we started the initial dive into assessing your management/leadership candidate. While that topic dealt specifically with discipline and termination, we now transition into the candidate's ideas, thoughts, and perceptions about what a leader really is.

I believe that a good way to start this deeper dive is to ask general and conceptual questions about leadership to open up the topic. Once you crack the door open you can ask more specific and hard-hitting questions about their history serving under leadership as well as how they have led others. You will find in the sample questions listed below a progression from general to specific.

I don't sense that I am to go into any great

detail on the topic of what leadership traits you are looking for in your candidate. There are a multitude of books written on leadership and I certainly don't consider myself an expert on the topic. Additionally, more than likely, you may have different needs than I or others would as it pertains to the specifics of the position for which you are recruiting. The main point I would like to stress is that you need to know exactly what you feel you are looking for prior to interviewing applicants. When you do that, it makes assessing your candidates less subjective and more objective.

- What, to you, constitutes being a good leader?

- In your experience, name qualities or characteristics of bad leaders you have worked for.

- How have you changed in the form of leadership as you reflect over your work history?

- In terms of leadership, specifically regarding strategy, how do you rate yourself? What are areas for improvement?

- What type of leader are you? How do you go about getting things "done?"

- How often do you solicit feedback from those that work directly for you to determine if you have any possible areas that you need to improve in?

- Describe what you have learned through this process (strengths and weaknesses).

# Chapter 36: LEADERSHIP PLANNING

Proverbs 21:5 The Message (MSG) **Careful planning puts you ahead in the long run; hurry and scurry puts you further behind.**

During the screening and interview process with your leadership candidates, understanding their ideas, abilities, and past performance as it pertains to planning, creativity, and strategy formation could be important depending on the specific position for which you are recruiting.

Below you will find some potential questions to ask of your candidates.

- What, to you, constitutes being a good planner, being someone who strategizes, and being visionary?

- In your experience, name qualities or characteristics of poor planners you have worked for.

- How have you changed in the form of planning as you reflect over your work history?

- Do you consider yourself to be a creative person? If so, how?

- With regard to this job, what are some of the planning and implementation elements you believe are crucial to launch as soon as possible to ensure success?

## Chapter 37: SELECTING ONLY THE BEST CANDIDATES AND APPLICANTS

Proverbs 13:20 The Message (MSG) **Become wise by walking with the wise; hang out with fools and watch your life fall to pieces.**

Proverbs 14:7 The Message (MSG) **Escape quickly from the company of fools; they're a waste of your time, a waste of your words.**

Proverbs 26:10 The Message (MSG) **Hire a fool or a drunk and you shoot yourself in the foot.**

As you are reading, studying, and applying the principles of Scripture as outlined in this book, you are becoming more knowledgeable, insightful, and hopefully more effective at the recruiting, screening, interviewing, and hiring process. I hope that you continue to hone your skills and abilities in these areas in order to give your business or organization the highest opportunity for success.

However, your self-assessment regarding your skills and abilities is not the most important topic to discuss here. In this particular section, you need to be able to assess the skills and abilities of the leadership candidate you will be interviewing. Specifically, you want to understand how historically effective they have been as it pertains to interviewing and selecting the right candidates. Most likely you won't be able to sit in on every single interview that your selected candidate will have to conduct in the future. As such, you will want to gain some level of confidence that your incoming leader has the ability to select the right candidates. Of course, I hope you will purchase them a copy of this book once they are on your team so they can continue refining their skills. But, at this point you need to assess what level of hiring proficiency your candidate possesses. In order to do that I suggest that, like Chapter 35, you use a progression from general topics on their theories and ideas about hiring into specific questions that drill down into their past experience in this arena.

The 3rd Proverb I have listed under this Chapter title is one that I take very seriously. For several years I have had the opportunity to speak to graduating seniors at several local high schools regarding what employers' expectations are for those that they are looking to hire. While I don't cite chapter and verse (Proverbs 26:10), I do state this is a saying or proverb that has great application. The bottom line is that hiring the wrong person can have devastating effects on your business or organization. This is certainly the case as you look to hire leaders and managers in your organization. As John Maxwell says, everything rises and falls with leadership. That being the case, apply these interview principles to ensure you hire the right candidate for each position for which you are recruiting.

- How do you go about only selecting the best candidates for any given open position for which you are recruiting?

- What are the key attributes, characteristics, qualities, and skills that you look for in candidates?

- At your most recent management/leadership position, how many people did you have working for you? Of those, how many reported directly to you?

- When you began in that role, how many of your direct report employees would you say were in the following categories? (taken from the concept of college football high school recruits being ranked with 5 stars as the highest ranking)

    - 5 star player (or 5 star potential)
    - 4 star player (without 5 star potential)
    - 3 star player (without 4 or 5 star potential)

- Were you able to change the "ranking" of any inherited team members? How did you go about that?

- When thinking about promotions, how did you go through the process of determining who should be promoted?

- Regarding staffing for positions, how did you go about finding and selecting people to fill those positions?

- Regarding new hires that you brought into the organization how many ended up being 5 star players?

- Regarding 4 star and 3 star players what did you do with them? (train, move, terminate, etc.)?

# Chapter 38: COACHING AND TRAINING YOUR WORKERS

Proverbs 1:29-33 The Message (MSG) **"Because you hated Knowledge and had nothing to do with the Fear-of-God, because you wouldn't take my advice and brushed aside all my offers to train you, Well, you've made your bed—now lie in it; you wanted your own way—now, how do you like it? Don't you see what happens, you simpletons, you idiots? Carelessness kills; complacency is murder. First pay attention to me, and then relax. Now you can take it easy—you're in good hands."**

My personal preference is to try all measures to promote from within the business or organization with which I am involved. This is most important to me with management or leadership positions. This process involves the need for a lot of advice, coaching, training, and mentoring. If you agree with my philosophy on this subject, you'll want to ask some of the following questions during the interview with your leadership candidates.

With these questions, your intent is to make attempts at understanding your candidate's proficiency with staff development. As you ask these questions you should begin to gain insight into the successes and failures your candidate has had with training, coaching, and mentoring past employees.

- Regarding new hires you have on-boarded, how did you go about ensuring they received the proper training needed to perform to your expectations?

- How do you go about writing individual development plans with all your direct reports?

- What are the areas that you have had challenges with regarding training, coaching, and development of workers?

# Chapter 39: ENSURING ACCOUNTABILITY FOR YOUR DIRECT REPORTS

Proverbs 13:10 The Message (MSG) **Arrogant know-it-alls stir up discord, but wise men and women listen to each other's counsel.**

Proverbs 13:24(a) The Message (MSG) **A refusal to correct is a refusal to love**

Proverbs 25:11-12 The Message (MSG) **The right word at the right time is like a custom-made piece of jewelry, and a wise friend's timely reprimand is like a gold ring slipped on your finger.**

In Chapter 34 we focused on the termination philosophy and process to which your candidate adheres. This Chapter focuses on discipline and accountability rather than the avoidance or adherence in the arena of termination. I do believe that we have the responsibility to try to address the difficult and problematic areas of our employees.

With the questions below you should be able to gain some insight into how your candidate deals with these difficult management or leadership responsibilities. The principles in the Proverbs listed above indicate that counsel needs to be given and received in order to be wise and loving, respectively. You do not want to hire someone that is a conflict avoider. Your business or organization will suffer as the sores that develop continue to fester without any salve being applied. On the other hand, you don't want a leader or manager who rules with an iron fist...I label those who operate under that principle as "management by intimidation." There needs to be a healthy balance between love and respect as we seek the workplace redemption of any employee that is not properly performing or interacting with other team members.

- When you have difficult subjects, items, or areas to discuss with subordinates, how do you address those topics?

- How have you ultimately dealt with those that could not achieve the stated goal or result?

- What was the most difficult situation you have ever had to deal with in this realm?

# Chapter 40: NAVIGATING CONFLICT

Proverbs 12:18 The Message (MSG) **Rash language cuts and maims, but there is healing in the words of the wise.**

Proverbs 15:1 The Message (MSG) **A gentle response defuses anger, but a sharp tongue kindles a temper-fire.**

As opposed to the previous chapter where we dealt with discipline, in this chapter we need to understand our management or leadership candidate's ability to conduct investigations, bridge the gap between, or reconcile those who are in conflict, and ultimately restore harmony and teamwork.

If ever there is a workplace topic that needs wisdom to be poured out upon it, surely it is the area of interpersonal relationships. I dislike workplace drama intently and my leaders know that we work to eliminate drama at all costs. It takes wisdom and gentleness to try and navigate these waters.

I want to understand, with my management and leadership candidates, how they approach and handle issues of workplace conflict. Or, do they even deal with it at all? Are workplace divisions ever given the attention they require in order to heal team morale and foster a positive working environment?

The questions below will help you begin the process of understanding how your candidate views and handles this topic.

- What was the most difficult situation you ever had to deal with regarding managing conflict among your subordinates?

- What is your approach or method to diagnosing, documenting, and determining the outcome from conflict among subordinates?

# Chapter 41: LEADING DEEP AND WIDE

Proverbs 25:3 The Message (MSG) **Like the horizons for breadth and the ocean for depth, the understanding of a good leader is broad and deep.**

In chapter 3, we discussed the concept of making inquiries of candidates in terms of what they are doing to grow, expand, and learn as a person or employee. Are they someone who is trying to gain knowledge, insight, and wisdom? In this chapter we are specifically dealing with management and leadership candidates. Without question I want to know how a management or leadership candidate is making an investment of time, energy, or resources to grow as a leader. I'm not just talking about reading books or taking classes. There are a variety of other ways for leaders to expand their horizons. I think about topics such as networking, learning facets of their business other than just what tasks they are currently charged with performing, and expanding their horizons in other verticals. You may have thoughts on related topics as well.

Another great learning tool is failure. Neil Kennedy has taught me that there are two ways to learn...the first is from personal failure and the second is from the failure of others. He suggests learning from the failure of others. A great way to do this is reading biographies of other people. Another way, already mentioned above, is to network and expand your circle of those that you know and from whom you learn.

The questions listed below should give you a starting point for diving into this topic with your management and leadership candidates.

- How are you growing or expanding as a leader?

- What examples can you give regarding past expansion (deep and wide) as a leader?

- If you think about areas where you made mistakes or failed with those that work for you, if you had it to do over again, what would you change and how?

# Chapter 42: WEEDING OUT THE WICKED

Proverbs 25:5 The Message (MSG) **Remove the wicked from leadership and authority will be credible and God-honoring.**

In a previous chapter we dealt with your management or leadership candidate's ideas and abilities surrounding termination. That was a more general discussion about all employees under your leader's scope of responsibility. That topic included all who fell under the umbrella of your leadership. Here, we want to specifically dive into your candidate's ability to deal with those that have a direct report relationship. Allowing direct report managers and leaders in your organization to operate in wickedness and unrighteousness will result in extremely negative outcomes.

The specific questions listed below will give you a glimpse into thoughts, ideas, and past performance as to what your candidate allows to go on in their business or organization.

- How have you allowed wicked people to have reign under your care?

- What has been the result of allowing the wrong people, who exhibit bad character, to remain under your charge?

- What steps have you taken, for accountability sake, to right the ship regarding having the wrong management team?

- What employees are in your organization now that are at risk due to wicked management?

- Is your turnover/retention negatively affected by not having the right people in the right seats?

# Chapter 43: WORKING UP THE LADDER

Proverbs 25:6-7 The Message (MSG) **Don't work yourself into the spotlight; don't push your way into the place of prominence. It's better to be promoted to a place of honor than face humiliation by being demoted.**

There are many memories (some good and some bad) that I recall about my first professional job upon graduating college. One of those memories is of a senior manager who wasn't shy about taking credit for someone else's work when engaging with those to whom she reported. It was the topic of discussion among many in my peer group that there was little respect for this senior manager. It appeared to many in the organization that she was trying to work her way up the corporate ladder by taking credit for the work of other people. There are many lessons I've learned along the way in my professional career, but this is one of the very first that I can recall learning. Since then, I have always attempted to give recognition to my team members for positive results, achievements, and successes. On the opposite side of the ledger, I try to insulate or protect my team when things aren't going so well. Now, that doesn't mean that underperformers aren't coached, counseled, and ultimately terminated if necessary, but I want to give them every opportunity to become successful.

My point in this particular section is, when interviewing leadership candidates, to find out what their history has been surrounding how they handle both praise and criticism. This assessment relates to how they personally receive praise and criticism as well as how they incorporate the team members under their direction when praise and criticism are given. Additionally, I want to come to some level of understanding how they received promotions in other organizations. Were those promotions a result of throwing someone under the bus? Were those promotions a result of taking credit for something that a peer or subordinate performed? Ultimately, you are attempting to discover what your candidate's teamwork skills are like.

The suggested questions and topics below should get you started on a path toward discovery about this section.

- Provide the account of the last positive situation, outcome, or result that occurred at work and how you received or accepted that praise. (Note: If not provided during the initial response, dig for clues about how they did or did not include peers and subordinates.)

- Provide the account of the last negative situation, outcome, or result that occurred at work and how you received or accepted that criticism. (Note: If not provided during the initial response, dig for clues about how they did or did not include peers and subordinates.)

- With regard to promotions you have received in other organizations, how did those come about? (Note: You are digging to find out if they are a self-promoter that has forced their way up the company ladder.)

- When were you demoted in a company, and why?

# Chapter 44: PLAYING FAVORITES

> Proverbs 28:21 The Message (MSG) **Playing favorites is always a bad thing; you can do great harm in seemingly harmless ways.**

As a manager or leader, playing the game of favorites can have significantly negative consequences on the morale and team environment in your business or organization. While there are most likely team members that outperform others, you trust implicitly to get projects done timely, accurately, and professionally, and that you rely on heavily; having the perception of treating certain team members as a favorite is dangerous.

Much like with parents who have multiple children, playing the comparison game between those that work for you is dangerous. As each child has a different set of skills, gifts, talents, outlook, direction, and calling, so it is the same with those that report to you in the work environment. The trick, talent, and skill set you as a leader must possess is to try and get the best out of every single person that works for you without the appearance of favoritism or preferential treatment. This is not an easy area to balance, implement, and oversee as a leader.

For this section of the interview, you are looking to find insight into how your managerial or leadership candidate is treating, and has treated, those under their authority. The questions below can help begin the process of digging into if and how this candidate could affect the morale and team chemistry if brought into your business or organization.

- Who is your favorite employee right now and why?

- How do you treat this person differently than others you lead?

- What impact is this favoritism having on your team?

- What have been the consequences of favoritism to you or others in organizations where you worked?

# Chapter 45: INSPIRING YOUR TEAM

Proverbs 29:19 The Message (MSG) **It takes more than talk to keep workers in line; mere words go in one ear and out the other.**

I've mentioned previously that I am certainly no leadership expert. However, I am trying to learn more and apply what I have learned in order to improve. One of the things I have learned throughout the years is that many I have had the privilege of leading responded well, appreciated, and respected the times when I was willing to learn the x's and o's of what my team members have to do on a daily basis. Additionally, from time to time, I have performed alongside them those tasks and responsibilities. I think it helped them to know and understand that I don't just push things off on them and that I'm willing to help out when needed.

I believe our Proverb for this chapter indicates that exclusively talking about something, not backed up by some tangible action, results in the message being diluted, rejected, or ignored. Of course, words are important, in my opinion. I try to make routine attempts at saying "thank you," "I appreciate that," and other expressions of appreciation. Am I perfect at execution in this area? Absolutely not!

However, during an interview for management or leadership positions, I believe that we need to grasp some insight into how the candidate is going to interact with, respond to, and inspire those they will be charged with overseeing.

- How do you inspire or motivate your team?

- What are your preferred methods of receiving appreciation and attentive leadership?

- In what ways have you struggled with employees not following through or executing on what you say?

# Chapter 46: CARING ABOUT WHAT OTHERS SAY ABOUT YOU

Proverbs 29:25 The Message (MSG) **The fear of human opinion disables; trusting in God protects you from that.**

This is a difficult topic to address. As our Proverb for this chapter indicates, you do not want to be crippled with fear as a result of criticism aimed in your direction. However, I do believe a healthy dose of reflection, introspection, and possibly changing course can be appropriate in some situations. Does this mean that you must (or should) shrink back, cower, or succumb to every suggestion, critique, or differing opinion that is directed your way? Absolutely not!

That is why I think it is important to come to some understanding of how your management or leadership candidate deals with these types of situations. As I'm interviewing for these positions, I'm looking for some level of balance in how the candidate interacts with those for whom they have responsibility. I believe the following questions will begin the process of helping you to come to some understanding about where your candidate lands on this spectrum.

- How do you deal with or let others' opinions of you affect you?

- How do you try to cater or pander to those people to change their opinions?

## Conclusion:

I hope that you have found significant value in the content of this book.  Additionally, my desire is that you believe there is deep application for you and your business or organization as you look to sharpen your interviewing skills.  While this book is not an exhaustive dive into the world of recruiting, screening, and interviewing candidates, I believe that it can unlock much wisdom, insight, and knowledge which will be necessary to guide you to selecting the right team members to fit the culture of your business or organization.

While I personally still don't get the right hire all the time, these principles have helped me to secure a better process to weed out some candidates that absolutely will not be a fit.  Where I might have decided to move forward with a candidate previously, the responses, answers, and insight gained through the interview guide and scorecard process developed from the wisdom of

Proverbs have helped me gain a much better, well rounded, and full scope decision making process.

Also, I don't pretend to be the absolute authority on the interviewing and selection process. It is always valuable for me to have others sit in on the interview I'm conducting or, if others are not immediately available, to schedule a time for others to conduct their own interview to gather insight for the purposes of comparing and contrasting information in the decision-making process.

I trust, hope, and believe that you will have much success as you work toward shoring up any areas of your interview process that, through this book, you have been able to identify as lacking.

In order for you to be made aware when I am going to publish the several books that are currently in the works, please subscribe to my page at:

www.subscribepage.com/j8c0g8

As a gift for subscribing to this page, I'll email you periodic, free, unpublished writings.

You can find out more about other books I've written on my website,

www.alanbalmer.net

Additionally, please feel free to contact me at the email address below for any questions you may have.

Email:
alan.scott.balmer@gmail.com